THE
INCREDIBLE
INCAS

THE INCREDIBLE INCAS

Yesterday and Today

by CARLETON BEALS

*Illustrated with photographs
by Marianne Greenwood*

ABELARD-SCHUMAN NEW YORK

Library of Congress Cataloging in Publication Data

Beals, Carleton, 1893–
  The incredible Incas.

  SUMMARY: Describes the Inca civilization from before the days of the Spanish
conquest to the present time.
  Bibliography: p.
  1. Incas—Juvenile literature. 2. Kechua Indians
—Juvenile literature. [1. Incas] I. Title.
F3429.B398   980.1   72–2077
ISBN 0–200–71901–7

Published simultaneously in Canada by Fitzhenry & Whiteside Limited,
Toronto.

Manufactured in the United States of America

10   9   8   7   6   5   4   3   2

Contents

Photographs

THE
INCREDIBLE
INCAS

The Shining Mantle 1

The People of the Empire

In the Andean highlands of South America a modern son of the Incas is herding llamas across the far-flung meadows. He is clad in a woolen jacket and trousers and wears a striped knit stocking cap that covers his ears because most of the year it is cold. Silent, he stands staring at the great snow heights or he plays his flute, a sort of five-note scale.

A daughter of the Incas sits beside a wayside shrine or runs barefoot along the trail with her newest baby on her back. Sitting or walking, she is always spinning llama wool on her twirling distaff, with its loose wooden, terra-cotta, or metal rings to guide the threads.

It was the same in the days of "The Inca." Today the word *Inca* has come to be applied to all the peoples. In this region, but long ago, it referred to the emperor and to the ruling nobility. The Incas established their supremacy over the Quechua Indians nearly a thousand years ago and built the great stone city of Cuzco, "the center of the world." Gradually, they extended their dominion for thousands of miles north to Ecua-

A modern farmer tending his land in the Andean highlands

dor and southern Colombia; south to all Bolivia, upland Argentina, and Chile; west to where the great peoples of the coast had built palaces and mighty irrigation works; and east to the delightful *yungas,* or valleys, of the Andes and on to the jungles of Brazil. One emperor sailed out with a large force to the Galápagos Islands in the Pacific, land of the huge turtles.

But the herdsmen and spinners, the farmers and artisans, the traders and warriors, the musicians and dancers of the great empire were Quechuas and allied peoples, the Aimaras and Collas of Bolivia and southern Peru, the Chibchas of northern Ecuador and other peoples of the coast and the jungles. Today

there are at least 20 million descendants all told, and most of them still speak their ancient languages.

Wherever the Quechuas and Aimaras go, or whatever they do, they are apt to tread the stones of ancient glories. As of old the spinning goes on, the llama herds still move over the landscape in the shadows of the great stone facade of Tiahuanaco in Bolivia. In Cuzco they trot past the curved eastern wall of Coricancha, the Inca temple, now a Dominican monastery, where in his day the Indian high priest sacrificed white llamas to the Sun, the God of Creation, on a great gold disc encrusted with jewels. The llamas pass by the greenstone cathedral that rises on the huge stone foundations of an ancient palace.

Women spin wool while caring for their children and crossing the highlands

The herdsmen not far north in the Andes may sit down to rest on one of the Incan lookout seats of Machu Picchu high above the Urubamba River whose rushing waters break in green white spray on rocks two thousand feet below.

The farmers of Huaylas in the far north, where in 1967 a terrible earthquake killed fifty thousand people, can clamber over the carved stone monuments of Chavín, a city built by their forefathers four thousand years before Christ. The power of early Chavín, whose people knew so many of the arts later practiced by the Incas, spread to the jungle and all along the

The mighty Urubamba River flows far below the heights of the ancient site of Machu Picchu

coast and on into the highlands, almost over the same area as the Inca empire five thousand years later. Today the farmer's plow or the digging stick may turn up old bones, stone idols, carved relics, utensils, weapons, and tools made and used by his forefathers of long ago.

When the Inca descendants climb the low sand hills to the old ruins of Pachacamac, south of Lima, at every step the grinning skulls of his ancestors leer up at him with empty sockets. Here and there, he traverses the ancient paved highway along mountain heights where the emperor used to be carried in gold- and silver-bedecked litters to visit the towns and cities or at the head of great armies to conquer new regions. They built balsas to carry them to the Galápagos or to take huge armed expeditions down the mighty Amazon tributaries into the jungle country.

The modern sons and daughters of the Inca sell their wares: beautiful textiles, pottery, carved gourds, fretted silver jewelry, clay animals and toys, and coca leaves in the vast markets of Pucará, southeast of Cuzco or central Huancayo and Ayacucho and a hundred other towns and cities. They sell images of the sun-god, Viracocha, whose splendid temple, in ruins since the Spanish conquest, was the very heart of Pachacamac, on the coast untold aeons ago. Sun fiestas are still held all over the country. It was the greatest fiesta of all in Inca days, when each year a gold chain was symbolically cast into the waters of Lake Titicaca where, on the nearby Island of Sacrifices , the Temple of the Moon, still stands.

Near Cajamarca, a mild spot in the northern coastal range of the Andes where Emperor Atahualpa built a summer palace, the huge stone baths of the Incas, into which the water boils in hot froth from the nearby springs, are still in use. So are the Tambomachay baths near Cuzco. But the stepped series of roads and baths at Machu Picchu, which seem so modern with their carved corner seats, stone handholds, and niches for cosmetics, are no longer working.

Here and there the traveler may pass over a chasm, thou-

sands of feet deep, on an ancient Inca suspension bridge slung
from massive stone towers, for the old thick fiber cables have
been replaced by steel cables.

To the Corpus Christi fiesta and the church on the hill
above Cuzco, just below Sacsahuamán, pilgrims flock from
hundreds of miles in vivid regional costumes. They wave
branches with white waxy leaves that flutter loose like butter-
flies and drift down like a snowstorm. They come dancing their
shuffling steps to the music of flutes, three-string guitars,
drums, and small harps. Most women wear skirts that reach the
ground, but some mountain girls wear tiny ruffled balletlike
rose-colored skirts that stand out from their thighs and bare
dancing legs.

Above at the massive stone fortress, some of whose foundations may be older than those of Cuzco, a family eats lunch on
the ancient polished Inca throne overlooking the wide parade
ground where the emperor in his robes and resplendent headdress reviewed his forces or awarded trophies to athletes. Here,

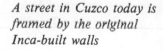

*A street in Cuzco today is
framed by the original
Inca-built walls*

in an elaborate October ceremony, he received the teen-age boy runners who came from a hill twenty miles away to prove their fitness as adult warriors.

On an outer massive battlement of Sacsahuamán, a Que-chua dangles his legs as he looks over the glorious golden city below with its mellowed tiled roofs and mighty walls, its churches and palaces, its great squares and gardens, crowded on this fiesta day with joyous people and religious processions. All the bells are ringing.

According to legend—the Shining Mantle legend—this unusual city was founded more than nine centuries ago by the first Inca emperor, Manco Capac, and his sister–wife, Mama Ocllo.

The First Inca

At dawn on a clear spring morning, Manco Capac, founder of the Inca dynasty at Cuzco, stood at the entrance to the Cave of Royal Windows and looked out over a wide fair valley of the upper Andes. He appeared there in a robe of gold—his shiny

The city of Cuzco as seen from the hillside below Sacsahuamán

mantle—with a golden staff in his hands, just as the early sun reflected the dazzle of his rich attire into the eyes of the awe-stricken people in the market below.

He proclaimed himself Son of the Sun, of Viracocha, the supreme god of the early peoples. He called himself the Inca, which also means sun, then hurled his staff farther than any ordinary man could, and where it buried itself in the deep rich soil he bade the people build a holy city.

It struck between two small streams flowing down from the Sacsahuamán heights, where the walls of an ancient fortress stood. The two streams joined below the heights to flow into great tributaries of the Amazon, then on to the Atlantic Ocean.

Exactly where the staff fell, the people laid out the Holy Plaza and the Joy Plaza of the new city, Cuzco, which was to become the most magnificent city of South America.

Over the next four or five centuries grandiose edifices were erected. Enormous blocks of tailored stone, sometimes twenty or thirty feet long, were fitted tightly to form the walls of palaces and temples. Stone aqueducts were built to bring in mountain water.

As the Inca empire expanded, roads thousands of miles

long were constructed, as were suspension bridges that provided crossings over chasms thousands of feet deep. Farm terraces were shored up with stones, tier on tier, to the snow line of the mighty mountains towering three or four miles into the sky. On the steep terraced slopes they grew fruit trees and corn and potatoes, beans and chiles, *oca* (an edible tuber), and coca, whose leaves were chewed for the cocaine and used for medicines and soothsaying. *Quina,* today called quinine, was used for fevers, particularly malaria.

By the time the Spaniards came Cuzco had grown to a city of 200,000 and the empire, with 30 million people, had a larger land area than Rome—larger than any empire before the Spaniards conquered the New World.

Little by little the Incas extended their rule over most of the Andean region, the upland plains, the coast, and into the edge of the jungles beyond the Andes. Their first expeditions took them through the central parts of Peru and Bolivia. From this core they moved on to the edge of the Argentine pampas and crossed the frozen Andes to occupy and administer Chile as far south as the Maule, where they were stopped by the warlike Araucans. They spread north through the mountains and along the coast, taking over all of Ecuador and part of southern Colombia. A flotilla was sent to the Galápagos Islands.

The Empire

The word *Inca,* today utilized to designate all the people they ruled, referred merely to the emperor and his relatives. They were the nobility, the "Big Ears," so-called, because they wore gold disks which distended their ears. The size of the disk varied according to the respective rank. In time a few outsiders were admitted because of brave exploits and ability, and, later, local officials who proved helpful and loyal were allowed to call themselves Incas and to distend their ears.

Except for the jungles of Ecuador, for fifteen hundred miles

In the colder climate of the highlands a boy keeps his ears well covered with a traditional Peruvian wool cap

the coast was a rainless desert, with vegetation only near the rivers that flowed down from the Andes, where numerous colossal irrigation systems brought water to fields of cotton, maguey, cereals, potatoes, corn, squash, sweet potatoes, yams, chiles, plants for seasoning, and herbs for medicines.

What otherwise would have been a blisteringly hot climate was eased by the icy north-sweeping Humboldt current, and was mild as far as the dense Ecuadorian jungles.

The foothills and western range of the Andes were also barren, with little plant or animal life. But the inner ranges had considerable rainfall and wide meadows, although there were few trees even on the higher plateaus.

In contrast, the eastern Andes, especially the slopes toward the Amazon jungles, were a true paradise of continual spring climate, with abundant rain, dense vegetation, a glory of flowers and rich soil. The *yungas* were and still are delightful valleys with twelve months of bloom and crops. Birds and animals abound.

The highlands are often cold, sometimes with deep snow, and there in olden times as today people lived in stone or adobe buildings and wore thick woolen clothing. Great tributaries of the Amazon, which drain two million square miles, rise in the frozen heights of the Andes, and cut through regular gorges to the Brazilian jungle. Down these rivers the Incas sent massive expeditions to invade the jungle country.

The Wonder City of the World

Over the centuries Cuzco became the magnificent stone city of Tahuantinsuyo, the Four Regions, as the empire was called. It was considered the center of the world—indeed, of the universe. Here the Incas, the Sons of the Sun, sat on a golden throne and ruled over the Quechuas—people who live in the canyons. The empire was tied together by fine roads and able administration, by the religion of the sun-worship, by trade and patriotism. The Incas were regarded with almost fanatical admiration, and when they moved abroad in their gold, silver, and turquoise litters, the people strewed flowers before them.

In Cuzco the Incas brought conquered chiefs to marvel and their sons to be educated. To conquered villages and cities they sent Quechuas to settle, to teach the arts and crafts and the language. There was constant interchange within all parts of the empire.

In the capital, the great Joy Plaza was for the people and their fiestas, their music and dances—jaguar dances, condor dances, warrior dances. The Plaza of Tears was the Holy Plaza where the priests performed elaborate religious ceremonies, such as the Tying of the Sun, a phrase which meant determining the equinox by dials or stone towers set for that purpose. Four wide avenues—later narrowed by the Spaniards—rayed out to the four quarters of the empire.

The oldest pre-Inca constructions (so old that no legends have survived) are found on Sacsahuamán, the Satisfied Falcon, on the hill above Cuzco. They are crude, but massive. Later the Incas added more defenses there, with truly colossal blocks of stone which had to be transported from quarries six leagues away.

The oldest important structure at Cuzco was probably Coricancha, Garden of Gold, a palace, fortress, and temple. Its eastern side, semicircular so that the morning sun could always penetrate the windows, was devoted to the worship of the sun. There the priests sacrificed white baby llamas, burned coca incense in twelve huge gold urns, and sprinkled holy water brought in by gold pipes to the large fountain of gold spouts— just as the dawn sun struck through to shine on a great gold disc encrusted with emeralds, turquoise, and chalcedony. The disc was a radiant flashing sun-face.

The Coricancha was part of a complex of structures called the Inticancha, Garden of the Sun. Originally the walls, especially those of the throne room, were covered with gold, which has since disappeared. Several other temples, parts of which still stand, were dedicated to the sun, the moon, Venus, the Pleiades, lightning, the rainbow, and thunder. The chief priest was called *Uilac-umu* (the head who counsels).

Offerings and sacrifices were made on the various altars: coca leaves, corn, potatoes, flowers, *chicha* (beer), *quinóa* (pigweed used as grain), llamas, and *cuyes*—a sort of edible guinea pig whose intestines were used for divination. Ex-votos of gold, silver, or copper in the form of humans, animals, or plants were presented. Fine clothes for the gods were also offered.

Subsequent Incas built individual palaces, most of which were enormous. Forts, museums, military academies, parks and sports fields *(canchas,* a word also meaning gardens or courtyards, still used throughout Latin America; viz., a modern *jai alai* court is called a *cancha)* made Cuzco an impressive center. Zoological and biological gardens had replicas of every plant, animal, and bird in the empire, modeled in gold. Relief maps of every part of the empire were exhibited.

Prisons, convents, and temples were built. Every street had

its altar or shrine. Chronicler Polo de Ondegardo counted 320 of them. Many of the greatest edifices were built by the third emperor, Yupanqui, who pushed the frontiers far and wide.

A schoolhouse for the sons of the nobility covered five square blocks. There they were taught religion, history, language, and the reading of *quipús,* the varicolored knotted cords on which were recorded statutes, history, the census, and, it is claimed, even poetry. The census was so complete that according to early chronicler Garcilaso de la Vega, the Inca emperor had a record of every pair of alpaca sandals beside every bed or hammock in the realm.

Garcilaso spoke eloquently of the "greatest and most superb" edifices that demonstrated Inca majesty and power. Cuzco seemed "reared by enchantment, by demons, not by men." The walls were more like cliffs; the gigantic stones had had to be transported over steep mountains and declivities by main force. How could they be fitted so accurately that the joint could hardly be detected? As Polo de Ondegardo summed it up: "That city of Cuzco was the home and habitation of the gods." Every fount, every wall, spoke of mystery, wealth, and power.

It was a city of towers and fortresses and imperial splendors, chained to the sun by golden links. The sun still rules there. The people were and are the Children of the Sun, worshipping at the mighty altars of the Andes in the temples of the dawn, temples in gardens of silver and gold and tumbling flowers.

Sacsahuamán

The third Inca, Yupanqui, had the main fortifications at Sacsahuamán built. It was a rush job on which four thousand stonecutters toiled. Six thousand men dragged the vast stones over the plain with huge leather and agave cables. Thousands more worked on excavations and the foundations. The stones, after being perfectly tailored, were moved into place, over tem-

An abandoned Inca city located in southern Peru

porary earthen ramps, with levers and ropes. The whole place, built to "last as long as the world," was a thousand feet long and six hundred feet wide. Some stones in its huge walls were as big as small houses, twelve feet by twenty. Some, as chronicler Cieza de León put it, were bigger than an ox and fitted so closely that not even a *real,* a thin coin, could be pushed between them. One stone, he said, measured 270 handspans around; it was so high "it seemed to have been born there." Had it not been so well dressed, one would not believe that it had ever been moved or that human strength was great enough to have put it in place.

Sacsahuamán was brilliantly engineered. Overhanging semicircular parapets with loopholes command every inch of possible enemy approaches. Beyond it an amphitheater and a highly polished throne, cut from granite, overlooks a broad level parade ground. Sacsahuamán was such a vast job that it was not completed even in the reign of the Inca's son, but was finally finished by his grandson.

Many winding stone steps lead up from Cuzco to Sacsahuamán. To this day multitudes of mountain people arrive on market and fiesta days from far and wide and dance over a sea of bloodred *muccho* flowers, to the wail of flutes, guitars, and harps.

At nearby hot springs, baths were carved from the solid stone. In an adjacent grove were the baths of the *ñustas,* the holy nuns, and men who ventured to peek were turned into stone by the goddess Caullaca. Two rivers ran between stone-walled banks through the city; in places they were and are covered by stone slabs. Other water was brought in by stone aqueducts.

Modern Cuzco

Modern Cuzco, thanks mostly to the ancient Incas, is still a majestic though sadly neglected city. Here and there modern doors have been opened through twelve-foot Inca stone walls and inside are houses—perhaps a barbershop or a grocery store. Censers swing in the notable greenstone cathedral which faces a small square and is erected on a massive Inca foundation. Spanish edifices with airy balconies perch like birdcages above powerful Inca walls. There are notable Spanish buildings, also, with great tiled garden patios surrounded by arcades and walls with frescoes centuries old.

A red flag and a bunch of red Inca flowers on a long bamboo pole is the sign for a *chicha* shop. One steps into a sunny Spanish patio. A dainty spiral staircase with its artistic iron railing leads to a second floor, colorful with glazed flower pots and flower boxes. The *chicha* shop, however, is an Inca stone room and has the usual bar and a few tables. Only the arched ceiling is fairly modern. There is the equivalent of an Inca pinball machine; a huge carved green toad. The game is to pitch pennies into its mouth. The *chicha,* a foaming sort of beer fermented from corn or

Some citizens of Cuzco stop to talk in the afternoon

potatoes, from peanuts or fruit, is served in thick green glass mugs. The favorite is that made from red berries of the *pirú* or *mollé,* the false-pepper tree.

The patrons are Quechuas, and they speak Quechua, as does all Cuzco. Spanish is heard only around the main plaza, in the tourist hotel, in the government palace and in the mouths of officers in police stations and barracks.

Much of Cuzco is wide and open. Vistas open up at every half step of large monasteries and convents and handsome modern churches. But part of the city is a tangle of narrow alleys. One steep thoroughfare is so narrow that one can touch the walls on either side with the fingertips. A donkey, loaded with a netted bale of charcoal, scrapes the walls on either side. Shouting warnings for a right-of-way, the driver sends the animal rushing down. The children and pedestrians have to dash into doorways to avoid being bowled over and trampled. The man is dressed in a wool cap, woolen jacket and shorts, with bare legs and leather sandals. His cheek bulges with a wad of coca leaves, which he keeps there continually and sometimes chews to release the cocaine and thus deaden his pangs of hunger.

The Indians are poor and often have little to eat. But the cocaine and allied alkaloid ingredients give him prodigious energy, for they prevent the body poisons from entering the bloodstream until he sleeps. In the morning he wakes half stupefied and must renew his coca chewing.

In Inca days, when the people had more to eat, coca-leaf production was a royal monopoly, and chewing was allowed only to people who had to perform incredible tasks—like the *chasqui,* or messengers, who carried royal orders over the roads, running in relays at top speed over the crests of the mountains, or to soldiers on the eve of battle.

The great market in Cuzco, as in older days, is a jumble of products and artifacts, great heaps of llama and alpaca wool and blankets, of carved gourds, black and gold pottery, fruits, potatoes, corn, beans, *quinóa, oca,* and other vegetables, and

Two Indians who are new in town seek employment

piles of coca leaves. No peasant leaves Cuzco for his fields without buying a week's supply of these leaves. Around his neck he carries a little leather or cloth bag containing the lime or *quinóa* ash with which it is always chewed, moistened with a little *aguardiente,* or firewater.

Coca leaves are also used for medicinal cures. Pasted on the temples, they drive away headaches. They are used for divination, foretelling the future and people's fortunes. Coca-chewing soothsayers can be hired for a joint cocaine session in which the fortune-teller chews rapidly to induce a visionary state, until he finally comes forth with a poetic recital of his client's forthcoming woes and joys. If the chewing is "sweet" the prophecies are bright, if "bitter," they are gloomy. Few serious matters are undertaken without consulting such a soothsayer. He usually begins by invoking the all-powerful sun-god, Viracocha.

One corner in the market is devoted to medicinal herbs and charms, quinine for fevers, digitalis for heart trouble. There are leaves and barks and roots for every malady known to man. Fetuses of llamas are bought to lie buried under the floor of every new building to insure a happy and prosperous household.

Everywhere people are driving camellike llamas, sometimes carrying light loads—the dainty creatures refuse to carry more than a hundred pounds. Before shearing, their wool—black, white, or brown—hangs in heavy curtains almost to the ground, giving them a tentlike appearance. In Inca days they were a royal monopoly, with great herds tended by specially trained herdsmen.

A Quechua in his woolen clothes, a small pouch over his shoulder and wearing earrings, leans against the the hotel wall, playing his flute, the *quena,* an instrument known long before the Incas. He plays on a five-note range, a monotonous dirgelike wail that answers the plaintive nostalgia of his being. He finds it satisfying, for he plays on and on, protected from the drizzle by the overhang of the eaves—all morning, all afternoon, on into the night. He plays with a sadness and perhaps with longing for the way things used to be before the empire of the Children of the Sun came to its end.

End of the Empire

In 1525, Inca Huayna Capac died in Quito, Ecuador, bequeathing the northern part of the empire to his illegitimate son, Atahualpa, and the southern part to his son Huascar. His heart and entrails were buried with elaborate ceremonies and his body was taken in state to Cuzco. For a thousand miles and more the roads were loud with wailing mourners. At each stage the notables joined the march behind the catafalque. Stops were made at each temple and shrine and in every village. Scores of llamas were sacrificed. Women who had pleased the emperor on his campaigns stuffed their mouths with leaves and died of suffocation, and it was said more of them perished than llamas that were sacrificed. His mummy was finally placed in the Temple of the Sun, along with those of his ancestors.

For a whole month his son, Emperor of the Faith Huascar, divested himself of his fine raiment and ate no spiced food. He fasted for long periods. Each day the arms and the emblem of the dead emperor were carried among the people, who chanted the praise of their lost ruler.

It was necessary, Huascar immediately perceived, to provide numerous additional royal officials for the expanded empire and he proceeded to have many offspring by the Holy Vestals of the Sun. But eventually he began to dream of further conquest and decided to go north to conquer the rich domain of the Chibchas in Colombia beyond Quito. There was no longer much profit in extending the empire in other directions.

In Chile the Incas had reached the Maule River below present Santiago, but beyond were the fierce Araucans. To subdue them would require a bloody, costly war with little hope of adequate rewards. In Argentina, the conqueror had reached the edge of the vast pampa, and that flat, low country demanded techniques the Incas did not possess. There, too, the rewards were meager, for at that time there were no domesticated grazing animals, the llama being a highland creature. The edge of the jungles had been penetrated via the Beni River in Bolivia and by other great streams, but the rewards from this sparsely settled and difficult region were better obtained by trade. Most of the coast had been won, and its highly civilized peoples added to the empire. But the Chibchas in Colombia were a rich people living in a rich land.

The barrier to northern conquest was Atahualpa. Huascar sent emissaries with a friendly but a firm message reminding him that as head of the empire he had the duty of conquering the peoples beyond Quito. He asked his half brother to recognize his authority.

Atahualpa, a canny man, sent back word in a friendly fashion, but proceeded at once to enroll thirty thousand men under his famous veteran general, Quisquiz. Thus prepared, he sent word he was coming to pay his respects to the emperor in Cuzco and to render due homage to the memory of their father and take an oath of fealty to Huascar.

Not until Atahualpa approached Tomebamba in the Cañaris country did Huascar hear of the powerful northern legions and realize that Atahualpa planned to oust him. He hastily assembled an army and spurred the Cañaris, the most valiant fighters in the empire, to resist. Their tradition of reckless valor availed little. Tomebamba was razed to the ground by General Quisquiz. While Atahualpa waited behind at Cajamarca, where he had built a handsome palace and royal baths, his general advanced rapidly to the mighty Apurimac River near Cuzco and crossed over.

A terrible battle ensued on the plains about ten miles from the capital. Atahualpa's forces were nearly broken, but by the

The wealth of Cajamarca is still evident with this well-dressed youth from that city

time red streams of sunset rode through the sky over the bloody earth, Huascar was in full flight. A conch shell trumpeter sent the victory message across the surging hosts. Quisquiz soon took Huascar prisoner.

The good news reached Atahualpa the next day. He donned the red vicuña turban, symbol of the ruling Inca, and set forth for Cuzco.

Meanwhile his followers were now busily seizing, torturing, and killing all of Huascar's relatives, including his wives and sisters. Huascar was obliged to witness these brutalities before finally being executed himself.

After all, Atahualpa was the older son and, in his own eyes and those of many, entitled to the throne. He now ruled over a territory of nearly 400,000 square miles, with a population of 30 million people. It was far larger than France and Italy combined. It was the greatest western land empire that had ever been put together by the greed and power and intelligence of mankind.

But before he made his triumphal entry into Cuzco, news came of the landing of the Spaniards at Tumbes on the coast, and he turned back to Cajamarca. There, not long after, in a single futile battle on a drizzly November afternoon in 1533, Atahualpa was himself taken prisoner.

From his prison quarters he watched the entire empire crumble as the Spanish legions moved on through the Andes and along the coast. He tried to ransom himself by having his subjects bring in large quantities of gold—a whole roomful—but the Spaniards, despite promises, laughed at him. The alleged room still stands. A red mark bands the ceiling, supposedly indicating the height of the gold amassed there.

In captivity at Cajamarca he learned to play chess well. Soon he was able to read and write Spanish. He studied the Christian religion. What spelled his doom, it has been said, was when he wrote the word *Dios*—God—on a fingernail and showed it to Pizarro; he discovered that his captor did not know how to read and write, and Atahualpa's scorn was so great, the conquistador was provoked into killing him.

2 *The Quechuas Today*

The people lived on in the ruined empire for a few centuries as vassals of the conquering Spaniards, then in a so-called republic, which they did not run. A subject people, they were forced to work on large *haciendas,* the best of their lands taken from them, and their villages reduced in size and importance. But the Quechuas have survived, still speak their own language, and are still struggling for their rights.

The Quechua was always a highlander. He made a tight personal and social knot with the Andes, from the foothills up to sixteen thousand feet above the sea. He still cultivates the valleys and the mountainsides intensively to the very edge of the winter snow line, which is lowest from June to August.

When the Spaniards came, they founded Lima on the Rimac River—that is where most of the Spaniards lived and still live, except those who ran the mines at Potosí, and Huancavelica, and later at Cerro de Pasco. Only since the airplane and the building of a few roads have the mountain Indians swarmed into Lima and other coast cities. Three-fourths of the people still live in the highlands. Most are full-blooded Indians —the rest largely mestizos living in Indian style. In the old Inca area, Quechuas, Collas, and Aimaras, all the descendants of the Inca empire, total 20 million or more.

In spite of a few modern roads, several railroads, and the airplane, much of the region has poorer means of communication than in the days of the Incas. The Incas found no natural barriers too great to surmount and they unified the whole empire. When the empire fell apart and the Spaniards closed in, the old Inca roads, not suitable for horses, fell into disuse. Villages were often left isolated. The peoples were fragmented and today are often more inaccessible than in ancient times, living apart in the deep gorges and valleys.

Only in the last few decades has there been a real revival of Indian unity, the emergence of popular will by the Quechuas, if not to control the country, to preserve their independence, free themselves from serfdom, and obtain lands. Three guerrilla revolts in the last decade were ruthlessly put down by the army, the leaders killed or jailed in the island prison off Lima. But the latest military dictatorship that took over has found it necessary to free them and break up many *haciendas* and distribute land. Today, after so many centuries of misrule and oppression, the Inca people are becoming citizens of the republic. Even so, they still live mostly by their old customs.

Women who are characteristic of the Quechua people

The Communal Ceremony

Don Joaquín Sameño bows his visitor, a neighbor, into his home in a prosperous little village, fourteen thousand feet above the sea, near Huancayo. The house is made of adobe—sun-baked bricks—with a red-tiled roof. The outside is calcimined a rose color. Over the front door extends a small tiled roof surmounted by a cross. The walls of the *sala,* or parlor, are painted deep blue up to a dividing line about four feet high and light blue above. The high ceiling is a slightly different shade of blue. A number of pictures of saints, Mary, and Christ adorn the walls. The floor is hard earth. There are no windows, no tables, only a plain wooden chest, several benches, an adobe wall-bench covered with alpaca blankets. A door leads to a bedroom with a *tobanco,* or bed, about three feet high, made of thin slats, covered by blankets and sheepskin robes. Below it are various carved gourds and terra-cotta receptacles. Another chest, this one carved, sits against the wall.

A corridor leads from the *sala* along the front of the house, with an adobe bench its entire length, facing a cage for birds.

A prosperous ranch surrounded by eucalyptus trees

At the far end is a granary, off which is a chicken pen. Diagonally across the open patio from the *sala* is a pigpen and the kitchen, with a few terra-cotta pots, a slanting coarse stone for grinding maize and a crude adobe firebox, over which is a smoke-blackened crucifix.

The garden and orchard are separated by another adobe wall. A large thatched structure contains cornstalks and fodder and tools. In a corral are three cows and at one end is a small triangular thatched roof under which they may sleep at night and can find protection against sun or rain. In the garden are grown corn, potatoes, *quinóa, oca, ullaca* (a squashlike vegetable), and broad beans. A corner is devoted to flowers—orange *sempasuchil,* carnations, a red rosebush, a cactus. A castor-oil plant and a flowering vine grow in one corner near a trash heap. Beyond there are a number of plum, peach, and cherry trees. The thin leaves of the false-pepper tree hang down gracefully. Tall eucalyptus trees line the rear of the property.

Don Joaquín wears leather slippers that enclose his heels and cover the front part of his feet, homemade stockings with a gray crisscross pattern, knee-length trousers, white drawers, a pink shirt, and a sleeveless vest. The trousers open on one side and have yellow buttons. When he goes out he usually wears a striped poncho and a flat-crowned felt hat. Today he is dressed up. He is receiving a visitor for a special occasion.

Don Gregorio Callante is the neighboring shoemaker, or better said, sandalmaker. He can make six pairs of women's sandals a day. The materials cost him forty-four cents and he sells them at sixty cents. This gives him a profit of ninety-six cents a day. Household expenses are partly covered by his wife's earnings. She weaves cloth and sews clothing on a rented sewing machine to sell in the market—shawls, shirts, and vests along with the sandals. But many days, when it rains, he may not sell a single pair. Even so, they usually earn enough for themselves and three children to eat, at a cost of forty-six cents a day, and enough to provide one outfit of clothing a year.

The two Sameño sons—one eighteen, the other twenty-one

—come into the *sala*. His wife, Doña Blanca, brings in *chicha* in terra-cotta cups. Her very wide, woolen skirt is ankle-length, her blouse free and loose. Over her shoulders, a bright-colored shawl is held in place by a silver pin. She walks noiselessly in a pair of goatskin shoes. Her long hair is parted in the middle and hangs down her back in two braids. She wears fretted silver earrings and a wide silver brooch with her initials. When she goes to market she puts on a narrow-brimmed, low-crowned felt hat encircled with artificial flowers. From the sides and back hang a short cloth veil to protect her neck and cheeks from the sun.

After the *chicha* has been drunk Doña Blanca and her two girls, thirteen and fifteen, bring in cups of sweetened thin gruel, made from toasted barley. On another occasion she might serve wheat and potato soup, seasoned with chile and boiled wild mustard leaves and stems. A similar gruel is made with roasted corn. Rarely is meat eaten.

As in ancient Inca days they have only two meals a day. The food is similar to that of pre-Conquest times, eaten in mid-morning and immediately before sundown, though a thin broth is usually taken just after daybreak. Fruit is eaten when in season. Much favored is the tuna, or cactus, fruit. People stuff themselves with food only on special market days or at fiestas.

Both Joaquín and Gregorio are *regidores*, assistants to the mayor, or *alcalde*, and they are discussing the village cultivation of the common lands set aside, as in Inca days, for the support of the civil authorities, and the preparation of the plot reserved for the church. All the villagers, men, women, and children, will take part. Such joint labor is called *aine*. This year a potato crop is to be planted, next year *ocas* or some other tuber crop, the third year barley.

Two days before—it is mid-March, just after carnival—the district governor had reaffirmed all the individual land titles with due ceremonies, a big feast, and the blowing of trumpets. Prayers, corn, and *chicha* offerings were made. Each owner was called up and paid a fee of a few cents; previously each had delivered a load of wood to the governor's house. A spade of earth was turned over at the corners of each property. The owner picked up a clod and kissed it.

At dawn the day of communal cultivation Joaquín and Don Gregorio set out carrying their adorned carved staff of authority. Doña Blanca and the four children carried the tools: a *chaquitoaclla,* a sort of spade with an iron blade and a side rest for the foot; a *taclla,* an adze hoe with a blade inserted in a forked stick; and clod crushers, heavy sticks with large stones tied tightly to their ends.

On arriving at the town land the villagers squatted on the ground and chewed coca. Joaquín then put his staff aside and started the work. He and his sons began digging the first row. The spade was thrust into the ground, the whole body weight was placed on the footrest and the sod turned over. Blanca and the girls seized it, divided it into two clods, which they broke up with the heavy crushers.

Soon the villagers joined in and the teams worked in regular rhythm, turning over each bit of sod simultaneously. Sometimes they accompanied the work with songs and timed their labor to the rhythm of the music. Labor was lightened by talk and jests or good-natured shouts.

After about an hour of hard labor Joaquín's and the other teams paused for another coca-chewing session. Joaquín then took up his staff again, but the other workers continued until noon, when all stopped for a lunch of dehydrated potatoes and cheese. After brief coca-chewing, work was resumed for an hour, when it was broken by another short spell of coca mastication, then continued steadily until five. With shouts of good-bye, all started homeward for their evening meals.

The second row of spading was made at some distance. Later crossrows were dug, leaving rectangles which were then spaded to make various magic patterns designed to insure good crops. Dates for planting are determined by the phases of the moon. The full moon is considered very unfavorable.

The work and ceremonies will be repeated ten days hence on the saints' lands, belonging to the church, at which the priest will replace the *regidor* as director. Later, much of the harvest will be devoted to celebrating the festival of the village saint. Harvest festivities are especially lively.

Joint labor is used to repair the irrigation ditches and in performing many village tasks on the various individual *tupús* during cultivation, sowing, harvesting. It was a brotherly way of life.

Picturesque gatherings occur at seed sowing—often done only by the women and children who also tend to the cultivation and weeding. Harvesting is done mostly by the men.

Special ceremonies are held in August to stave off sickness and injury to the crops. Coca leaves selected by the women are mixed with llama fat and incense and burned, and the ashes then buried by some of the men while everybody looks the other way.

Hail, very common in the highlands, is conjured away by incense burning and holy water. Bonfires are lit to discourage frost. When it comes anyway, it is because it is enraged by the attempted resistance of the Indians!

Destructive insects and gnats are thought to be the spirits of men who have injured or are malevolently injuring the community, and hence are excommunicated—not a very effective insecticide.

To bring rain, children sing the *"Misericordia"* and weep in the dry field. In earlier days children and dogs were sent to the fields to make a great din whenever lunar eclipses occurred.

An Elopement

It was springtime in the village in the Apurimac valley, just after the fields had been planted, when young Cusi Suchi abducted lovely Linda Sumac. He was a strong tall young man, handsome and bold, and she was the fairest girl in the village. As was customary, he brought her to the home of his parents,

Children of the Apurimac valley carry religious offerings

two of the more prosperous peasants with a well-built house and large garden. Trial marriage is an established custom among all the Quechuas.

Belatedly, for this should have been done before the abduction, his parents visited her parents. At first, Papa Sumac was very angry, and he berated them and their worthless son. They accepted the insults meekly, telling him that the couple were very much in love, that it would be a happy and beneficial union of two important families. Their son's intentions were serious; he should be forgiven for being so impetuous; after all, Linda was very beautiful.

They had brought gifts, more lavish than customary: a bottle of *aguardiente,* of which Papa Sumac was very fond; a large amount of corn and *chuño*; and what was less customary a fat sheep, which in a few months could be sheared. After more sputtering, Linda's father allowed himself to be pacified. Words of goodwill and esteem followed, soon seasoned with laughter and sly remarks about lovemaking.

The first step toward marriage had been taken successfully. The rest would depend on how well the trial period turned out to be. For many months Linda shared Cusi's *tobanco* and performed her share of household tasks, dutifully obeying all the orders of her future mother-in-law. She was sweet, humble, and competent in cleaning, cooking, spinning, and sewing. She joined in the freezing and trampling of the potatoes to make *chuño.* She fed the animals in the corral; she weeded the garden.

Such trial marriages are nearly always made permanent by a formal ceremony. On the strength of his approaching marriage, as in Inca times, Cusi was awarded his *tupú* of land; Linda had a right to half a *tupú*. This was duly recorded with the district governor.

After they had had a child, a boy named Rafael, he too was awarded a *tupú,* to be held in trust by Cusi till he married. In all, these parcels amounted to about four hundred by three hundred feet, considered enough to support a family of three. They also had rights in the village water, commons, pastures, and forest land.

Sheep and pigs graze around a country farmhouse in the Andes in the Apurimac region

Well before marriage, Cusi and the other villagers erected the couple's new home. He first consulted with the aged soothsayer, who threw coca leaves in the air and made his findings after carefully examining how they fell. He decided on which day the work should begin, just where the house was to be built, and the direction it should face. After the adobe bricks had been properly baked in the sun, a village fiesta was staged, with music, food, and dancing. The soothsayer mumbled prayers to Viracocha and burned coca leaves at the corners of the property. Under the future doorway, a llama fetus was buried. Thus all the prerequisites for a happy and prosperous household were fulfilled.

The walls went up quickly. Rafters were laid. Coarse *ichú* grass was tied in bundles, hoisted onto the roof, and properly laid down until two feet thick. A crucifix and an image of San Carlos were put in the proper niches, and the priest came and blessed the house amid general festivity. Coca was chewed;

chicha was drunk. Many *anticuchos,* chunks of lamb or innards roasted on bamboo spits, were eaten.

All told, the materials for the house cost forty *soles* (about five dollars) which was less than the expense for food and drink.

On Santiago Day formal marriage was celebrated in the bride's home with much feasting, music, and dancing. The women wore many skirts of varied colors and, when they whirled around, the skirts flared out like rippling rainbows.

The married couple left while the dancing was still going on, and returned to his parents' home. His mother locked them in their room. Presently the musicians, followed by the guests singing songs, continued the fiesta at his house, serenading the couple all night long.

The New Household

Little *cuyes* soon ran squeaking around Cusi's new home. Life was good for the couple, for all villagers here have their own land. During the last few years, the new government of Peru has seized many big estates and given land to the peasants. Now there is enough room to grow what is needed for each family, with a surplus for the market. There are many sheep, pigs, and a few llamas. The people of the village are very poor according to modern standards, but they are certainly more fortunate than the *yanacones,* or serfs, on the big haciendas. These have to work for the *gamonal,* or owner, for a few *centavos* a day and scarcely have enough to eat. The *yanacones* survive by chewing coca, for lack of sufficient food, and often suffer and even die from malnutrition. In the free Apurimac village coca is chewed for pleasure rather than for need.

By April Linda is carrying little Rafaelito on her back, slung in her shawl, next to the clod crusher on her shoulder. Cusi walks ahead with his iron-edged spade. In the field, Linda lays the child and her spinning in a blanket in the shade of a pepper tree.

At all hours of the day and often at night before going to bed, Linda twirls her spindle, making wool yarn. She is adept at it, often tossing the spindle almost to the ground and letting it climb back spinning to her hand.

The sod of the field is quickly turned over and crushed with the aid of neighbors. Since the land is on a fairly steep slope, cross-furrows are made so the soil will not be washed away. Higher up, Cusi had already started building stone terraces, where he will plant coca and fruit trees. He might, perhaps, try planting wheat, a new crop, which does well in this coldish climate and provides a white flour for bread, which tastes better than either the *quinóa* or the corn bread to which they have long been accustomed.

While the neighbors take a rest period and chew coca, Linda feeds Rafaelito. In a short time he will be toddling out

A girl from Andahuaylas in the Apurimac country

to the fields with his father, where he will work with miniature tools to help with the weeding and the digging of potatoes. In a few more years he will have his share of coca leaves and sack of *quinóa* ash, to be moistened with a few drops of *aguardiente* for the chewing.

Soon he has a sister, Malú, a gay little creature. "She's a heart killer," says Cusi, delighted with her. In a few more years she will be toddling about, carrying dishes and firewood and spinning her spindle. Another half *tupú* of land is awarded to the family—so they now have three *tupús,* a generous amount.

The children play few games. The girls are given dolls, sticks with nobbed heads, for which they make their own dresses and with which they play house. The boys build little replicas of the big house and plant miniature gardens. Sometimes the boys blow up a sheep's intestine for a balloon. They have a hard ball with which they play catch or which they toss against a wall.

All learn the fiesta dances early and have their own bright fiesta costumes. They whirl about with solemn, intent faces. It is a great joy but a serious holy business, so it is improper to display pleasure. They love to dance, as do all the children and grownups in the village. Special dances are carried on for each occasion—for the saints, the old gods, and the civic celebrations, such as Independence Day. There are many bird and animal dances.

Malú squeals with delight when she manages to catch a *cuy* who squeaks with fright but quiets down when she strokes its silky hair. The little *cuy* loves the lettuce and other leaves she feeds it, nibbling greedily with sharp teeth and bulging eyes. She loves to fondle baby pigs and sheep, too. Cusi bought several llamas and the frisky baby llamas make fine playmates.

Growing up Today

Just before the birth of a child, the mother and father fast. She confesses to a priest and prays before the household god.

She is given steam baths with chile, tomato, and incense, and her body is massaged with coca and *aguardiente*. Often the mother is attended by female relatives or a midwife, but on occasion is unassisted at the delivery. Professional midwives are paid about twenty-five cents a day. As the pains begin, the midwife presses the mother's abdomen and pulls her neck and feet to hasten the birth.

The newborn baby is tied loosely in a shawl and put in a cradle until able to crawl. For six months it is bathed every day in warm water, after that with cold water to make it stronger.

It is weaned a year or so after birth and an elaborate hair-cutting and nail-clipping ceremony is held with relatives and friends. The hair trimming is usually performed by the oldest uncle, who then gives the child the name it will use until adolescence. A new name is bestowed at the time of the ceremonial puberty initiation.

Early schooling is provided by the parents. Some localities have male and female clubs where boy and girls are instructed in moral and physical virtues.

The father patiently and seriously educates his son. At an early age, the child is taken to the fields where he is taught to care for various tools and is given light tasks. Girls are taught household duties by their mothers with similar care. Parents, grandparents, aunts and uncles, older children, give them daily instruction in spinning, weaving, and sewing.

Eighty percent never learn Spanish or how to read or write. Enormous areas of the highlands have had no public schools.

Schoolboys from the coast of Peru play games before going home

Not until 1972 did the Peruvian government begin setting up schools all over the country and teaching the people in Quechuan rather than Spanish.

At fourteen a boy receives a loincloth and goes through two weeks of exercises. In October the mother makes him a new outfit and in November he makes pilgrimages to sacrifice a llama and pray. The priest draws a line on the boy's face with llama blood and gives him a sling with which to kill birds and small animals. As in Inca days the customary footrace is staged, a dash between the mountain and the village.

A girl, in a later celebration, goes through less elaborate ceremonies. She fasts for three days, is bathed and has her hair combed in a new style by her mother, who dresses her in new, appropriate clothes and provides her with a new name.

When a child gets sick, a sorcerer or healer, male or female, is called in. The healer enters the sickroom with coca, sugar, a sheet of blank white paper, and a bottle of *aguardiente.* Twenty *centavos* are placed on the table or a bench. The "doctor" puts the paper on the floor, darkens the room and whistles three times to bring the mountain spirits, who enter through the roof and assemble on the sheet of paper. One spirit brings a dove said to be the cause of sickness. Another spirit strikes the curer and the child, eats the sugar, takes the twenty *centavos,* lights the room with candles or resin-wood torches, then departs. Sometimes the child is rubbed with red clay, black clay, then blue clay. The three clays are put into a vessel filled with boiling urine and the healer determines the cause of the illness from the vapor. Sometimes, however, a *cuy* is beaten against the sick one, then is skinned and its entrails are examined as a means of diagnosing the sickness. All this goes back for centuries. There are no regular trained doctors.

Children's Fiestas

Corpus Christi is an important occasion for the boys. The priest picks out a boy to visit all homes carrying images of the saints to remind people of the coming holiday. A Dawn An-

Children of the Sun pose for a traveler taking photographs

nouncer, a youth of eighteen, assembles the band of masked musicians who make the round of the houses at daybreak, singing *mañanitas* to wake up the people for the fiesta.

Boys take charge of the various dances and ceremonies, for which privilege they pay a fee of about fifty *centavos*. Five youthful *mayordomos* provide the music, food, and drink during the day.

Boys of fifteen to sixteen are responsible for the church music and a dozen of them perform the Dance of the Savages. Each must pay six *soles*. The leader is assisted by "one who cries out," that is, shouts the commands for the steps and turns, as in an American square dance. A twelve-year-old is captain of the year. He pays a set amount for food and drink, plus forty *centavos* toward the Mass.

Sheep are blessed on St. John's Day. Bonfires are lit at the gate of the corral. Young dancers, in teams of eight, go from house to house and dance to the music of a *charango,* or mandolin. The dancers are treated to *chicha* and *aguardiente.* The festivities last all day and night. The sheep are then blessed with *chicha,* coca, and *aguardiente.*

Llama blessing takes place on Santiago Day. The animals are given small amounts of *chicha.* St. Mark's Day is the day for blessing cattle. *Aguardiente* is poured over them and coca is offered to the mountain spirits.

Food

The chief food of every highlander's diet is the potato—particularly dried potatoes, or black or white *chuño.* Treading potatoes—part of the dehydrating or freezing processes—is performed by all members of the family. The potato fiesta are featured by offerings of coca and *aguardiente.*

Black *chuño* is made from selected potatoes, which are left to freeze on open ground, where they are sprayed with water at regular intervals. For several days the potatoes are alternately frozen and exposed to the sun. They are then trampled to eliminate any water that remains, after which they are covered with reed mats or sacks.

White *chuño* is made from bitter potatoes that are kept under water for several weeks until they become pallid. After the water has been pressed out of them, they are frozen. When defrosted they are repeatedly pressed, often with rocks, until dry. They become a white, chalky substance which is stored in llama-wool sacks, usually in special huts. The *chuño* flour thus made is used for gruel, soups, and stews *(chupes).*

Potatoes not dehydrated are first cooked, then frozen. Similar freezing or dehydrating is done with corn, wheat, *oca,* barley, squash, and *mashua,* a nasturtium tuber. Probably half the vegetables produced are preserved in this fashion.

The potato comes close to being the Peruvian staff of life. The greatest number of species is found in Chiloé Island, off the coast of southern Chile, where it was possibly first domesticated. It had spread over a continent and a half before being taken to Europe and then brought back from Ireland to the United States. Hundreds of varieties are found in the highlands, particularly in Bolivia, of every shape, size, and flavor—fat, thin, round, cubic, rectangular, oblong, twisted, white-fleshed, yellow, red, violet, gray, and black. Some are hardy right up to the snow line. These are mostly bitter and are utilized chiefly for making *chuño.* There is only one white-flowering variety, and it is a big yielder.

Most potatoes have twelve chromosomes, though several high altitude varieties are pentaploids with sixty chromosomes. But the much cultivated frost-resistant *lucci* is a triploid, that is, has thirty-six chromosomes. Five primitive potato species

Farm workers wash the season's crop

have survived in Colombia, Ecuador, La Paz, Cochabamba, and the eastern Andes. In Peru, the most widespread, with the best yields, are the tetraploids (forty-eight chromosomes). A widely distributed variety in Peru and Bolivia is the jet-black diploid *chapiña* (twenty-four chromosomes), used chiefly for dyeing, not for food. The white-flowering *papa amarilla* is the most prized of all Peruvian potatoes. Its golden flesh is highly nutritious and has a tasty nutlike flavor. White potatoes are considered fit only for pigs.

Next to the potato, the *oca* has been the most important root crop. It can be grown from cooler lowland areas up to the highest fields. Peru has five sweet varieties, eaten either raw or cooked, but it is usually sold dried in the markets. It has a chestnutlike flavor.

Widely distributed in the mountains is the *ullaca,* a climbing vine with an edible potatolike tuber called the *papa lisa.* It is red, yellow, or multicolored, full of starch, but very insipid.

The *mashua* is too biting in flavor to be eaten raw. It is supposed to make men forget their wives and was fed to soldiers by the Incas.

The *maca* or *maguí,* a shrub with edible leaves, good also for winemaking, and tubers, has always grown in the very highest and wildest parts of the Andes. The tuber is pearly white and is dried to the size of a small pear. Boiled or roasted, it is sweet, but so exhausts the soil that it can't be grown again for ten years.

The nightshade family provides tomatoes, nicotines, and datura. The last two have been used for centuries as drugs for religious ecstasy and prebattle excitants.

Much prized is the melon pear depicted in ancient pottery. Its flowers are purple, like those of a potato. It is halfway between a cucumber and a melon.

Cactus leaves are diced, stewed, and eaten. The flavor is insipid unless highly seasoned. Cactus plants also provide food for cochineal insects, which provide red dye, and have always been grown with much care in the Huamanga valley in central Peru.

Peppers or chiles of many varieties were and are cultivated or gathered wild. The *roccota* pepper of Peru is purple flowered, the fruit globular.

Corn, the sacred food of the Incas, grows in altitudes as high as 12,700 feet around Lake Titicaca and on terraces above Puno. It is widely cultivated—the entire length of the Vilcanota or Urubamba valleys, west of Cuzco. A special knee-high variety is grown in Ecuador.

Corn first attracted the early Quechua for its oil-rich pollen and the tender ears were eaten in the immature milk stage. In ancient days corn was often used in rituals and by soothsayers, and still is. Tender ears are used in harvest festivals.

Russian scientists have pretty well established that maize was originally domesticated in Colombia and spread north to Mexico and the United States and south as far as Argentina. The corn grown in the Andes is mostly flint corn and very resistant to insects. A hawkbill type, with curved kernels that point upward and hollow cobs, is grown around Cuzco and Quito, where it was probably introduced by the Incas. The early Quechuas made popcorn from a special variety that is still available.

At higher altitudes grows an amaranth, the bright-colored *quinóa*. It is a high-class pigweed related to spinach, found all over South America, and used since time immemorial. Today, it has become more important and productive than corn. A small ricelike grain, it can resist some frost and yields grain abundantly, but needs much nitrogen fertilizer. The grains are threshed out and are easily preserved for long periods. Some grains, large and white, are bitter and have to be repeatedly washed before being cooked or ground for meal. They are used for making *chicha*. The white or red leaves and stalks are cooked with oil, vinegar, and sugar, and the mixture is used to relieve stomach pains, colic and sore throats. In the north, it serves as a laxative and to augment the mother's milk. It is also used as a massage for mothers after childbirth, and as a paste over broken bones and tumors. In Cajamarca it was given as an enema in the treatment of typhoid cases. The Piurans in the north near Ecuador believe it is good for the gout. In Aequipa the ground seed is used with water to whiten and beautify the skin. The ashes from the stalks provide the alkali used in chewing coca. It is used for offerings to the old gods and on Christian altars.

The allied ash-colored *canihua,* another species, resists more cold than the true *quinóa* and requires less fertile soil, but is less prolific. It grows as far north as Mexico. Mostly it is roasted and ground to be mixed with water on trips. It makes especially powerful *chicha* and the people of Peru eat the stalks, with vinegar, for spider bites. In Arequipa it is taken with sugar to prevent mountain sickness or seasickness. At one time the Spaniards prohibited its cultivation because of its use in religious ceremonies. It is still sold in markets, often in small sweetened cakes with pink or blue coloring matter. *Canihua* was particularly favored by the Huanacas, a Quechua people west of Cuzco, and was and is cultivated intensively in valleys near Ayacucho, Huancavelica, and Apurimac.

Beans were much used in early Quechua diet. A large bitter type, a lupine, called *tarhuí,* is often planted in alternate hills with corn. It withstands cold and flourishes in poor soils. It has to be soaked several days to become palatable. It has been supplanted mostly by broad beans and field peas.

Peanuts, much used in the highlands, are grown in warmer valleys.

Scores of species and varieties of squash and gourds are cultivated and are an important part of modern diets. Seeds are often toasted and chewed as a between-meal snack. Squash blossoms have always been fried as a delicacy.

A sort of cucumber gourd is eaten green as well as cooked. Seeds have been found in ancient tombs, and the plant is depicted on the earliest pre-Inca pottery, thousands of years old.

A man in Ecuador cuts squash for cooking

The bottle-shaped gourd called *purú* was often depicted in ancient pottery. From the beginning gourds have been used for cups, dippers, ladles, water canteens, receptacles, and often bear beautiful designs of plants, animals, musicians, warriors, and fiestas. They also serve as floats for pontoon bridges.

There are innumerable fruits. The sour sop and the *chirimoya* are cultivated in lower valleys. They were depicted in Mochican pottery two thousand years ago. The black cherry *(Prunus serotina)* was also known thousands of years ago and is still grown. *Myrtacae,* a sort of cherry, has long been used in fruit drinks. Highland *papayas* are grown up to ten thousand feet and are gathered wild in Loja Province in Ecuador. Various *guayavas* are grown almost everywhere there is water. The *lucuma,* a species of sapodilla, is shown frequently in ancient pottery and stone carvings.

Roots have always provided a dependable source of food. The Incas imported sweet potatoes (a species of morning glory) from the eastern valley. Yams, which can grow at very high altitudes, apparently were brought in by early slaves from Africa. *Malanga* or *taro* is grown in warmer valleys. The leaves serve as greens, especially liked with fish dishes.

Coca, to this day a multi-million dollar crop, was the "money" of the highlanders, according to chronicler Juan de Montuzo, who wrote, "to ask that there should be no coca would be to decree that Peru cease to exist and the country given up."

It is set out as two-year nursery plants in beds. The forest is burned off and the fields are meticulously weeded. The leaves are gathered four times every fourteen months. The expansion of this crop was restricted by the Incas who permitted its use only for limited religious and military purposes and for divination and soothsaying. But its cultivation was spread widely by the Spaniards and today nearly every highland Quechua is a chewer.

Ever since early Inca days black *chonta* palm wood, which is very hard, has been imported from the Amazon jungles for building purposes and to make clubs and spears. Other tropical woods, yellow red, red, or black, are also brought in. Except along the rivers, there is little timber in the Andes, only the false-pepper tree is widely distributed and, since late last century, the eucalyptus has spread widely over the country. Its wood is not very useful except for burning.

Cotton

The ancient Peruvians mainly used as fibers wool and cotton and *totora* reeds which were woven into matting, baskets, and boats. The coarse fiber from the agave served then and since to make ropes, cord, coarse thread, and for sandals. Agave burlap was used to wrap mummies. The same materials are widely used today.

Cotton was brought in to the highlands from trees and shrubs in the valleys on both sides of the Andes where it grew wild. Seeds were eaten and had medicinal uses. It is the only four-chromosome cotton in the world, found nowhere except in Peru, Chile, the Marquesas, and Fiji.

At least three kinds of wild cotton grow in the tropical areas of the upper Amazon, in Piura Department in the north, in Ica and elsewhere on the coast. The coastal cotton, a perennial plant, living for twenty years or more, grows twenty feet tall. It also grows in Ecuador, up to the eight-thousand-foot level.

Father José de Acosta described it in 1588, "Cotton also grows upon small shrubs and great trees, like little apples which open out and yield this web, which is gathered and spun to make cloth. It is . . . of greatest profit and greatly used, for it serves them instead of both flax and wool to make their garments. It grows in hot soil, and there is a great amount on the seacoast of Peru. . . . The great store . . . is in Tucumán [on the northern coast] and in Santa Cruz province in the [northern] sierra. . . . They make cloth commonly used by both men and women, table napkins and . . . sails for their boats. Some [cot-

ton] is coarse; other is fine and delicate. They dye it into diverse colors, as we do our woolen cloth in Europe."

His "great trees" were probably ceibas common in northern Peru and in Ecuador, which give a silky cotton known as kapok in modern commerce. Thomas Cavendish, who went around the world in 1586-1588, observed that the people of Puno, high country in the south, used ceiba cotton. In earlier days the ambassadors of newly subdued Tucumán in Argentina, brought gifts of cotton cloth to conqueror Inca Viracocha, who took the name of the Sun God.

Pedro Gutiérrez de Santa Clara wrote as early as 1550, "There is in this country much cotton, naturally blue, brown, tawny, and yellow, the color so delicate it may not be noted, as though it had been dyed a long time, for the Painter of the World gave it those signal colors."

Cotton was deseeded by hand, then bundled into convenient lots for carding or combing. Combs of all sorts are found among Inca burial mounds and in caverns.

Animals

One of the most useful animals for the Quechuas, in Inca days and today, has always been a species of guinea pig (*Cavia porcellanus*) called the cavy or *cuy,* a small tailless rodent encountered from Patagonia to the Guianas, Central America, and Cuba. They have the free run of nearly every humble household in Peru, Bolivia, and Ecuador, living off greens and table scraps. The *cuy* weighs about two and a half pounds, and its silky, sometimes curly hair is white, brown, black, or grizzled. It has four front-paw toes and three rear-paw toes. The female bears from three to six young ones and produces four litters a year. The life-span is about eight years.

Originally it was free of diseases, but in this century became susceptible to bubonic plague. Thousands were destroyed by officials with resultant grief, bitterness, and violence on the part of the owners.

A boy petting his sheep while his sister looks toward the flock

The meat has a chickenlike flavor, and the animal plays a part in medical cures and religious ceremony. The warm viscera of a freshly killed *cuy* is laid on the abdomen to relieve pain. Many are sacrificed in air, water, and sun fiestas.

Iguanas have also been long valued for their tender white flesh.

Regular wild animal hunts are staged, as in Inca days. Deer, puma, jaguars, foxes, wolves, monkeys are driven into traps and killed. Birds are trapped or killed: tinamous, partridges, ducks, geese, toucans, parrots. Most homes have macaws, parrots, and other birds as pets, not always caged.

Wool is obtained, chiefly in the highlands, from *guanacos,* llamas, alpacas and the smaller wild vicuñas, all camellike animals. The finest wool, lovely and silky, comes from the vicuñas. Next in fineness is that of the alpaca, which before being dyed, ranges from white, blue, gray, tan, light brown, orange, to dark brown, and black. The bright yellowish wool of the viscacha, a large long-tailed rodent of the highest Andes, is used to vary the colors of undyed fabrics. It was originally used only for the Incas. Human hair was often utilized to give gloss and beauty to woolen cloths.

Both wool and cotton were woven all over Peru long before the Incas, which attests to a far-flung, well-organized trade in very ancient eras.

Weaving

The fineness, great variety, and intricate patterns of ancient and modern weaving are partly due to the manual dexterity so characteristic of Quechuas.

The picture of a textile establishment of the pre-Incan coastal empire of Chimú is shown on a pottery jar dating probably about A.D. 500. The workshop is under a thatched roof. A richly dressed woman, aided by a servant, is cooking meat. Other vessels contain fish or fruit. Smaller ones contain drinks.

Three weavers are at work, two of them copying the pattern of several rugs. The one in the center is composing a new design as he weaves. On another jar, the work is presided over by a richly attired warrior wearing a turban, with an ax head on it. He is being fed by a tunic-clad servant. Two other figures are singing to the warrior. Five weavers are shown, one of whom is composing an original design. Familiar designs were fruits, animals, warriors, sometimes in battle, priests, musicians.

The distaff for spinning, today as in ancient days, is a finger-shaped stick about a foot long with an open ring at one end into which the carded wool is inserted. Other rings of pottery, stone, bone, or wood, the length of the distaff, serve to guide the wool. The spindles are carved with beautiful designs, sometimes painted. The cotton is drawn from the upper ring by the thumb and forefinger of the left hand and moistened in the mouth, then threaded through the other rings. The spindle is then hung at the waist or as low as the knees and twirled. Various early chroniclers described the women and children all over the Andes, spinning as they went to market or herded their llamas, just as they do today. The spinners sometimes toss the spindle almost to the ground and as the wool winds about the shaft, it climbs back to the hand. When they are seated, the spindle is rotated in a bowl or a work basket. Before being woven the wool is washed to remove the grease and oils.

Simple handlooms have always been used to weave. The warp is held at the bottom by a heavy bar, sometimes tied to a belt worn by the weaver, who is thus able to draw the threads tight by leaning backwards. For longer pieces of cloth, two large bars at each end are attached to notched stakes, four to six feet apart—the warp being stretched horizontally. The cloth is rolled about the nearest bar as the weaving progresses. In some instances only one set of stakes is used; the weaver sits, kneels, and finally stands up as the upper fixed bar is neared. The width is from two to four feet. Narrow looms, sometimes only half an inch wide, are used to make girdles, fillets, bands, and straps.

A Puno mother and child portray the pride of their Inca ancestors

The weft is worked through the warp with the fingers. Small rods are inserted to separate the warp threads and make the insertion of the weft easier. Sometimes a spindle, usually of *chonta* wood, is used as a bobbin.

The fibers are usually dyed before weaving; only small pieces of textiles are dyed later. Today most dyes are synthetic and bought in the market. Some changes in weaving were made following the Conquest, although modern weaving is about the same as in pre-Inca periods.

Clothing

Clothing is also similar, though the loincloth is not common today except in remote villages. But skirts or tunics to the waist or knees, capes and sandals, are similar, often identical, with those of ancient times. The headdress in early Chimú days, before the Incas, was a cap or hat or a cloth that hung down behind to protect the neck from the sun. The women still use this. The early peoples also often wore animal skins with real or imitation heads and used the feathers, wings, and tails of birds. Among the Nazcas, further south on the coast, costumes consisted of a loincloth, long flowing girdles, a triangular cape knotted over the chest, sometimes a short-sleeved short shirt, a cap or bonnet.

The coarsest llama wool is worn by the lower classes and used for rugs and bedding. In Inca days the finest vicuña or viscacha wool and bat skins were woven by the Chosen Women or Virgins for the emperor and nobility. Robes were also made of bright feathers. Sometimes clothing was adorned with gold, silver, or copper, shaped into spangles and tiny bells, arranged in attractive contrasting patterns. Inca Viracocha invented a new type of brocade.

Now, as in those days, a bag hangs over the right shoulder and rests on the left hip. Incas and nobles wore gold and silver armbands and chest adornments, gold and silver or feather ornaments, and headbands of braided or woven fillets, with red and blue feathers making a crown. A red tassel, worn in Cuzco and by pre-Incan Nazcas, sometimes hung over the left temple.

The woman's tunic was wrapped around the body under the arms like a sarong and held in place by a fan-shaped pin and a broad woven sash. The tunic reached to the calf or the feet and opened up the side as high as the thigh when she walked. The Spaniards, though not a modest people, were so shocked, they made closed skirts obligatory.

The mantle or shawl, called a *lliclla*, still widely used, is held by a brooch. Over their hair is a cloth folded so that one end hangs over the forehead, the other over the back. Sometimes it also shields the cheeks.

Leather sandals are usually shorter than the foot in order

to allow the toes to grip the ground. The thongs are leather or strips of thick wool.

People at Work

Notable present-day weavers of shawls and ponchos, and others who knit shirts, stockings, and caps, live in Cochopata, a district of the mountain city of Ayacucho, "Corner of Earth," formerly known as Huamanga, "Hill of Condors." It lies in the foothills of the snowy Andes on the little Toroillo River which soon joins the nearby Mantaro—a thrice removed tributary of the Amazon—already at ten thousand feet, a mighty stream as large as the Hudson at its mouth. It flows between stone mountain walls.

A narrow grass-grown cobbled street dips down from the Ayacucho Plaza de Armas to the weavers' town. It runs alongside the cathedral and university and between massive convent walls, built of stones rifled from ancient Pocra temples, some of which predated the Incas. Even in those early days they were supplied with water by stone aqueducts. The tiled roofs beyond are covered with moss, for they, too, are rather ancient.

The weavers live on the narrow side streets before one reaches the tangle of sheep and llama corrals and the fields that slope to the river. Boundaries are marked by rows of lanky peeling eucalyptus and pencil-leaved *molle* trees. Across the river are fields of agave which provide fibers for fishnets and rope.

The women sell the textiles in the market, but many customers come directly to the weaver's house and, after a drink of *chicha* in the dark *sala,* are conducted to the patio. Under a thatched roof, on cross poles, are the varied products of the work, fine woolens as tightly woven as English cashmere, striped or checkered, some with designs. Some are made into ponchos, rugs, and blankets.

The primitive handlooms are pegged in the patio, though

Women of the Ecuadorean jungle wear clothes to suit the warm weather in rainy weather they are transferred to sturdy posts under an open thatched *ramada*. At both ends the horizontal pegged loom has bamboo poles which are tied to stout posts. The horizontal pegged loom is used mostly for making coarser materials.

Formerly family wool was obtained from homegrown animals. Today it is mostly purchased in the market. Often, the hide of a sheep is bought, the wool cut off, and the hide cured. The wool is spun, cleansed of grease and dirt, dyed by dipping it into *ollas,* or wooden troughs. It is then washed in decomposed urine, then in clear water.

Before beginning a new piece the weaver chews coca; this, he says, will prevent the yarn from being eaten by insects or rotting. He beats the yarn with a small black stick to make it more limber. He never starts a new job on a Tuesday or Friday, for that would bring bad luck. Most weavers will not let any outsider observe the weaving for fear that they will lose their deftness and skill.

Often the wife weaves also. Their boy, if he is over seven, helps out by untangling the yarn, supplying the alternate colors as needed, bringing *chicha* or toasted corn to munch, or chasing out the squeaking *cuyes* when they become a nuisance.

The weaver keeps track of the design by counting the number of threads. One artisan is a short broad-shouldered man with a big mop of glistening black hair, a black moustache, dark protruding eyes, a large nose, and strong chin. He wears a slate-colored shirt with a round collar, knotted at the waist like a sash, with the sleeves rolled up. His long brown-striped trousers have patches on the knees. When working he is barefoot.

The blanket, which will take about three days to complete, he hopes to sell for about twenty *soles,* a couple of dollars or so. Most scarves and ponchos sell for half that amount. After deducting the cost of his materials, he and his wife will jointly make less than a dollar a day.

Tin Miners

Four hours by car west from La Paz lies the village of Colquiri and one of the oldest tin mines in Bolivia. The highway leads up in corkscrew curves from the slot in which La Paz lies, to the bleak, almost barren, plateau above the capital; it passes by some of the most magnificent snow mountains on earth, among the highest in the whole Andean chain. It is spring and the peasants in bright costumes are cultivating their fields.

Hours later, the car reaches the rim of the valley where Colquiri nestles beside a small stream under a high mountain. The road winds down past a little plaza with its statue of a national hero and into the dismal town: a single street with a few stores, a newspaper stand, a bus stop, and several boarding-houses. Most of the squalid adobe or thatched houses where the miners' families live climb up the mountainsides. The large handsome structure beside the river is a clubhouse, formerly used by the foreign managers and employees where no Bolivian was allowed to enter. After the mines were nationalized, it was turned over to the miners. Along the side of the mountain is a seven-story reducing plant, which pounds and belches out smoke.

One stocky miner, an Aimara, on the eleven P.M. to eight A.M. shift lives in one of the hillside shacks with his wife and two children, both small boys. Every night—and nights are cold at this high altitude—he enters the mine and walks down a slanting gallery alongside narrow-gauge tracks for about three-quarters of a mile to the lift which will take him into the depths of the mine. About a third of the way in, a large grotto, which serves as a chapel, is brightly lit, with a glittering altar on which is the miners' patron saint. He pauses there, drops on his knees, crosses himself, and prays briefly.

At another grotto near the lift he checks his poncho, for the mine below is hot as central Africa except when ice-cold air is

The children of a tin miner stand by their family's home

blown in at points where work is going on. This extreme differ-
ence of temperature may partly account for the high incidence
of tuberculosis. He puts on his steel helmet, surmounted by an
image of the saint and a lamp that is powered by a heavy battery
strapped to his back. He takes the lift to the third level where

another grotto serves as an infirmary, with a surgical table and shelves of medicine. The doctor takes his pulse and temperature and gives him some pills in a small envelope.

At the fifth level, a really enormous grotto serves as the mine office. Here are desks, typewriter tables, and rows of metal files. It is connected by a passageway to the supply rooms, with neatly labeled bins of nails, spikes, bolts, screws, light bulbs, fuses, and other electrical materials. There are ropes, belting, hoses, nozzles, couplings, lengths of pipe, wire, tools, hammers, shovels, picks, crowbars.

At the sixth level a dump-car train is being loaded. A slanting, almost vertical, shaft runs from the top level to the lowest level, through which cables haul scoops filled with ore down or up to be loaded onto the train. This runs through a tunnel that comes out at the upper floor of the reduction plant where the ore is delivered to be stamped and pulverized. It is treated with acids and chemicals in great vats. Other metals such as gold, silver, zinc are drawn off. The final tin concentrate is shoveled into sacks to be transported by rail to Arica, Chile, where it is placed aboard vessels for refineries in England and the United States.

The miner has to wait a spell, for the lift is taking down lumber and timbers for a new tunnel on the ninth level, nearly a mile deep, which he is helping to open up. There he mans an electric drill to bore holes for dynamite to break into a new lode.

The strewn rock, some still in huge slabs, is broken into more uniform slabs by chisels and sledgehammers, then wheelbarrowed to the nearest track where it is hauled to the chute to be taken up to the sixth level.

At three in the morning he wipes the sweat off his face and neck and goes to the hallway of the office four levels up, where he sits down on the stone floor and leans against the wall, munching his meal of cornbread and bean paste. Afterward he dips coca leaves in his pouch of alkaline *quinóa* ash, sprinkles them with *aguardiente,* and chews them. They happen to be sweet, and his face grows contented. The coca leaves quiet the remaining pangs of hunger, numbing his stomach and stopping the absorption of poisons from his tired muscles. He is given a feeling of strength and well-being.

In the morning he trudges from the lift to the exit near the town. Through the cold outside air he climbs up the steep path to his small adobe house that clings to the mountainside. It is half covered by a red flowering vine. At the doorway are chickens and a small pig. A few *cuyes* scamper across the floor. He curls up on a mat to get some sleep, dozing off with the steady pound of the smelter in his ears and smoke from the stacks drifting into his nostrils.

He earns about a dollar a day with which to clothe and feed himself and his family. He must pay eight dollars a month for rent. He speaks Spanish poorly and has never learned to read or write. On his day off he goes to the clubhouse or the downtown union hall where he listens to the radio. A literate fellow worker reads the news. In this way he knows what is going on in the outside world about which he has acquired a deep interest and decided opinions. He knows about Viet Nam, Cuba, Chile, Egypt, and the Near Eastern war. He is probably better versed in Algerian and Asian politics than are most U.S. citizens.

His lot has bettered slightly since the government took over the mines. Formerly he earned only sixty cents a day and had to work fourteen hours instead of eight. At the government store he can now buy food and other supplies more cheaply. He has greater job security and belongs to a union, something previously not permitted.

He is not a Communist; there are only half a dozen among the several thousand miners, but he worships Fidel Castro and admires Ho Chi Minh and Mao Tse-tung and more recently Salvador Allende, for he feels that they have helped free their peoples. He is aware of the new freedom in Africa and parts of Asia, knows about the problems of Blacks in the United States. He considers this country the enemy of human freedom everywhere in the world. He knows that President Barrientos, who drove the elected President Estensorio Paz out of Bolivia, was

A young boy works to help care for his family

a general, dancing on the puppet strings of the C.I.A., the
American Central Intelligence Agency, which he blames for the
murder of Che Guevara. The C.I.A., it has come out, also has
bribed top Bolivian union officials. Barrientos was soon killed
in a plane crash, and a government more favorable to the min-

ers took office, only to be succeeded by a fascist military coup. He recalls the time when he and the other miners fought the federal troops from behind the rocks that ran red with blood. There was much killing, and he knows that any day now fighting will flare up again. His rifle is well hidden, but he keeps it in shape for future use.

He has not much energy left, after his hard toil, to do much about things. Even so, in his free time he is an artist and works on small canvases whenever he can afford a few cents for paints. He records scenes from the mines and the town. Once, on his day off, he painted all night to make a picture as a gift to a speaker at the union hall to show his gratitude for the message of freedom he brought. This particular day he stirs in his sleep as the muffled thud of a dynamite blast comes from the mine, and he listens drowsily to his boys and a playmate planning to go down to the river and wade among the reeds.

Hat Maker

A hat maker lives outside Soccoscocha in the Arican foothills of southern Peru in a thatched house with wide eaves. He buys most of his wool, or rather his wife does. She also helps with his work and sells the hats in the market.

They wash the wool carefully with soap to remove all grease, and hang it up in the sun. After it dries they shred it —that is, make it "flower"—by beating it with a taut vibrating cord of thick *cáñamo* fiber, held in a five-foot bow. The shredded wool flies into a heap near the wall. It is treated with a gummy vegetable substance to reduce it to a sort of paste, then is subjected to heat from an adobe firebox, covered with a sheet of copper or zinc, a baking process during which starch and more vegetable gums are added.

The felt sombrero is shaped on a wooden form and dried again in the sun. Then it is pressed with a hot iron. His wife adds an inner leather band and an outside ribbon, usually a light cream color. When enough hats have been made she trots off to market with them. They can make about two hats in a day and a half, and the profit is about seventy-five cents. They can make a bit more if they can buy wool on the hide. The hide brings in a few cents, more if cured.

Curing the hide takes a week or so. It is first soaked in water, then is treated with lime to get off all remaining wool. It is placed in a tank with vegetable material, usually from the acacia tree. Afterward, it is scraped with a knife-shaped stone or bone. It is washed again and allowed to dry in the sun.

Pottery Makers, Silversmiths and Carved Gourds

The most famous pottery in Peru is now made in Pucará, which is between Cuzco and Puno. The clay is good in the region, and many types of utensils and jars, decorative and religious objects, toys, receptacles, animals, and money banks are made. The whole family works, from toddlers to grandparents. The clay is fragmented, powdered, and made into smooth dough. For the very popular black pottery, the clay is dyed before being shaped and baked. The wheel is not used; the forms are shaped skillfully with the hands or on molds. The objects are dried in the sun and when almost dry the desired designs are painted on: animals, birds, plants, human figures, ancient battle scenes, fiestas, musicians, flute players. The jars and plates and toys are then baked in a small adobe oven. This entire process takes about three days. A few artisans know how to glaze their wares.

Some of the famous Pucará terra-cotta products are fat bulls, used as flower vases, banks, or toys, the prancing Santiagos, and various animals, such as pigs, panthers, jaguars, deer. Fiesta masks are also made of terra-cotta: devil faces with writhing serpents. There are condor, eagle, and jaguar masks. Other masks are made of papier-mâché.

Silverwork

Peruvian silverwork is superb. The artisan traditions go back to the earliest Inca days. Filigree jewelry, apparently spun by blowing, is lacy and exquisite, if often fragile.

The Quechuas are specially talented in engraving gourds with intricate pictures of animals, birds, plants, and human scenes, Inca warriors, battles, orchestras, dancers, popular legends, and religious themes. Sometimes the designs are burned on. The gourds are painted red, black, yellow, and green, and are highly polished.

The Huancayo Market

The great Sunday Huancayo market, one of hundreds throughout the Andes, is attended by multitudes of people—especially on fiesta days—some of whom travel through the mountains for weeks to get there. It covers about seven square blocks on two plazas. In one plaza, animals, cattle, horses, pigs, sheep, llamas, alpacas, chickens and other fowl are sold.

The people are less colorfully dressed than in Mexico or Guatemala. The men's clothes are customarily dark trousers or shorts, with shirts and coats in gray, brown, or black. Occasionally a light poncho has a bit of color. They wear dark felt hats. Men from higher counties wear wool stocking caps with earflaps. The women are mostly in dark blue, a dark skirt, a white, gray, or brown blouse. However, their shawls—usually wool, sometimes cotton, worn over their shoulders and backs—are often bright with variegated colors.

After laying out their wares on canvas, sometimes on newspapers or wrapping paper, in symmetrical piles often in artistic designs, they sit immobile, their ample skirts covering their crossed legs like a large circular tent. They rarely change position, though in the textile section, they sometimes rise, holding

An Ecuadorean selling his wares in the local marketplace

Ecuadorean girls sell melon by the slice

up a blanket better to display it and to point out the excellence of the weaving and attractiveness of the designs.

A tourist picks out a large fat gourd, polished black and red. The lid has a dozen irregular points and notches which fit snugly. The seller watches him intently. If the buyer makes futile efforts to refit the lid on, she knows he is unfamiliar with the article and doubles or triples her price. The knowing person always looks for the key—a flattened point that fits into a flattened notch, and thus puts the lid back on in its proper place at the first try.

A small man has a heap of viscacha pelts. After much lamenting of how much effort it cost to hunt them high in the mountains and cure them, reminding the buyer that they have become very rare, he will sell a dozen of them, enough for a fine fur cape, for a dollar or so. The curing is not very expert.

An old woman sells medicinal herbs in the city market

Numerous posts display great heaps of coca leaves. Nearby are piles of potatoes and *chuño*. Vegetables are piled in large mounds; green or shelled beans, oca, ulluca, tomatoes, chile peppers, garlic, yams, *malanga* or taro roots. Though very insipid, these are much used in Peru, also in Cuba and the Amazon. The corn seems rather stunted, with small cobs and small kernels.

The fruits displayed are rarely first class, though they have a finer flavor than better-looking varieties: plums, cherries, peaches, *sapotes, chirimoyas,* avocados, bananas, oranges, lemons, limes, mangos, huge orange varieties.

Candy is available. Sweetened *chuño,* or potato flour, is a favorite. The flour itself is frequently used with sugar to cover other fruits, custards, and puddings.

Open-air restaurants under thatched *ramadas* are numerous. Stews, soups, and meats are cooked over adobe stoves in big *ollas,* or foods are fried or toasted over flat tin grills. They give forth pungent odors, very strange to outsiders. Some eating places cater to special regions. Arequipan food is highly spiced with much chile. Many stands sell only *chicha* or fruit drinks.

Most goods are bartered for, but wares that come from afar usually have to be bought with money. This is often true of coca leaves, most fruits, salt, sugar, cotton goods. All are important for the Quechua. In general, prices are a thirtieth to a hundredth or even less than corresponding prices in the United States. A hundred pounds of white corn sells for about a dollar, other varieties a bit more. A pound of beef brings about five cents. Fine large onions sell for about two cents each. A felt hat costs from twenty cents to two dollars.

These prices reflect the fact that the Quechuas and Aimaras, if very poor, are all but self-sufficient. Few products have a fixed money value. Handicrafts are done in idle time between planting, weeding, and harvesting, hence any sum above the cost of materials that the maker can get is considered profit. Some artistic gourd carving requires incredible patience and time, so the low price has little relation to the labor time spent.

A variety of fruits are prepared for the market

Most Quechuas are pretty much outside the so-called money economy of modern times.

Obviously the marketplace does not wholly represent commercial enterprise, but is also a social gathering, a place for enjoying conversation and contact with others. Bartering or selling is a loved process, today more vocal than in Inca days. The seller usually asks two to four times the final selling price, which is arrived at only after prolonged negotiations, which delight both parties. The higher the original price, the longer the pleasurable time spent in bargaining. The sellers become versed in character and psychology, know just the right moment to cede a point or to become arbitrary or indifferent.

When the price is set high, the seller usually invites discussion, "I set the price high so you can make an offer and we can deal. I wish to deal with you."

If the buyer shows signs of leaving, the seller will say, "Offer, offer, make an offer! We are doing business."

Bargaining gives opportunities for wit, repartee, strategy, acting, and pretending, and provides emotional satisfaction.

3 *Children of the Sun*

Divination and Death

Soothsayers are found in all Peru. The supplicant presents himself with an offering of magical llama fat in which are stuck tiny flags, paper ribbons, figurines, animals, miniature tables, and farming implements. The diviner invokes the mountain spirits who are welcomed with handclapping and who tell him the name of any enemy or thief or other evildoer who has injured his client. The spirits, who come very long distances, must be paid and fed. Coca leaves are tossed in a shawl. Events are foretold by the pattern they make. Everybody chews the leaves. If they are "sweet," it means good luck; if "bitter," bad luck. After the seance the diviner burns the ashes of the leaves in llama fat. "Now the earth is content," they sing. In this way, the seal of approval or disapproval is placed on the harvest, marriages, travel plans, business ventures.

Death among the Aimara of Bolivia is announced by a bonfire and wailing. Relatives and friends bring food, liquor, and coca to be consumed during the wake. The life history of the deceased is recited and his virtues extolled.

The diviner breathes on the body with aromatic herbs in order to placate Mamapacha, the Earth Mother. If unmarried, the cadaver is shrouded in a white woolen tunic; if married, the deceased is dressed in coarse black. The man is buried in his poncho, the woman in her skirt and shirt. A string of llama wool is tied about the dead person's neck to signify the person is really dead, free of all worldly affairs and from suffering in the next world. Sometimes the string is drawn tight and the belly pressed with heavy stones to prevent post mortem flatulence. A white male llama is tethered to the dead one's hands, to be his companion to the other world, then is slaughtered and the meat eaten by the mourners. The hide is used to make sandals for the death journey over the rough road between earth and heaven. Food and a twig broom are placed in the grave to which the corpse is carried on a litter. The pallbearers trot rapidly, for the dead soul is eager to enter the grave and start on its journey.

At the grave site of a dead youth, an old woman, to hide her sorrow recites over the body in an angry tone.

"Coward, you are leaving this world in order not to face the responsibility of taking a wife and supporting children. You are like a rocky field that yields nothing." She then slaps the dead boy's face.

Clods are shoveled in—"messages to the departing one." The grave is deep and the earth is pressed down compactly, so none is left over to tempt hungry Mamapacha to devour some other person. All adults and young children jump over the grave so no sickness from the deceased will strike. The mourners turn their serapes, shawls, and jackets inside out and, after much drinking, stumble back home, always by devious routes to prevent the dead spirit from following them. They wash their hands and mouths and continue feasting for eight days.

The diviner, if available, or an old person, thoroughly cleanses the house of the deceased. The dead person's clothes are washed and burned or given to others. All present are immunized by burning herbs and chile.

A widow must mourn for a year and show no interest in the other sex. For three years, each November on the Day of the Dead, food offerings are made, one day for dead children, the other for dead adults. The days are featured by fasting, drinking, and varied religious rituals. People dance on the graves in bright fiesta clothes—a symbol of life's victory over death and disaster.

Traditional Dances

High in the Andes nestles the little rose-colored city of Huancavelica, built of cinnabar, for this was a mercury-mining center since Spanish days and perhaps before. People are performing their traditional condor dance in the plaza. The dancers are dressed to simulate the great bird. They have tail feathers and wear condor masks with long yellow beaks. The dancers imitate the flight, the lofty gliding and soaring of the majestic king of the heavens. They swoop down on their prey and rise up victorious. The music simulates the music of the spheres. The dance is a soul-escape into the freedom of a heavenly paradise.

In Aparú in the central sierra west of Cuzco a fight between a bull previously enraged by wounds, and a condor made drunk with *aguardiente* is staged. The condor turns on the bull with beak and claws. If the drunken condor flies up in a straight line, it is good luck. It has been said this is a symbolic fight in which the Inca's sacred bird wins the victory over the Spanish beast.

The condor dance is one of thousands, ancient and modern. The sun dance is performed at the spring solstice. Other dances are in honor of Mamapacha. One dance is held in worship of the mountain spirits; others satirize the Spanish Mass. Most, over the years, have been accepted by the church.

Each village has a distinctive dance for its patron saint. Dances for the Virgin Mary are frequent. The dance of Judas is celebrated on All Saints' Day. Many dances are in honor of

Women dancing together at a Bolivian fiesta

civic and patriotic events, such as Independence, the liberation
battle of Ayacucho, the holiday of heroes when a special war
dance is performed.

The largest number of dances relate to the farm life, the
fixing of boundaries, the plowing, sowing, and harvesting. The
women dance with tender ears of corn wrapped reverently in
their shawls, clutched to their breasts like babies to be placed
on the altars.

There are special dances for weddings, childbirth, puberty, and death. They tell of joy and sorrow—by moving the feet and body, and by music, but not words. There is the dance of the hungry and homeless in rags and broken hats. Notable is a dance of the hunchbacks in which neighbors are satirized and savage quips are exchanged. The dance of the rich satirizes the *gamonales,* or landowners.

In other communities, turkey and eagle dances are performed. The eagle dance is a war dance. No other country has a more varied and widespread dance tradition than does Peru.

Fiestas

In southern Peru the treading of grapes for wine, a sort of dance with lifted skirts, is performed to music made by a drum and accompanied by singing. In the grape fields, too, fiestas are held. The dancers refresh themselves with wine asked for in song. Often it is unfermented grape juice to which *pisco,* or brandy, cinnamon, and lemon juice have been added.

In the highlands, while treading the potatoes during freezing and *chuño* making, and similar fiestas, the drink is more apt to be *chicha.*

In llama country there are llama dances by boys and girls who tend the herds. The llamas are adorned with colored wool and small bells; the music is provided by *quenas,* or flutes, and drums. The music and the steps imitate the movements of the llama.

In Ichú, a village near Puno, the women carry tall poles, adorned with colored wool and topped with feathers, inside a circle of men playing flutes and bearing drums. The men wear feathers in their hats and white cloths pinned to the backs of their black coats. Some are dressed in animal skins and masks that imitate vicuñas, llamas, sheep, foxes, or jaguars. Sometimes they carry stuffed animals. Usually the dance is performed on a mountaintop and simulates a hunt for a lost animal. The soothsayer invokes the mountain spirits and the earth mother and sprinkles *chicha* over the ground. He sends forth dancers disguised as foxes and monkeys to recover the lost llama. There is great grief over the loss until the animal is trapped by the long poles. He is brought back in triumph. After prayers and thanksgiving they pretend to kill, cook, and eat him. Actually, toasted corn is usually substituted for the meat. It is a joyous banquet.

In the fiesta for the Virgin Mary, her statue is carried on a tall pedestal covered with white cloth and flowers. The women strew yellow wild flowers in her path. Dancers follow her, then musicians, important people, and finally the villagers. The image is carried under adorned arches to four altars at each corner of the plaza, where prayers are said. Flowers are tossed down from adjacent balconies and windows. Dancing continues all afternoon. The full-colored skirts swing wide.

Eight days later is celebrated the dance of the Inca. It is rehearsed in homes for weeks ahead. The procession is headed by a tall youth in a white robe, a bright striped cape, and a gilded crown. He is attended by richly clad courtiers. Everybody dances to the music of accordions and wooden flutes, down from an arch on the hill to the two plazas, then on home.

In Paratín, another Peruvian village, each dancer carries a small drum about his neck, which he beats with a wool-adorned stick and at the same time blows on a double panpipe. It is music said to have been played at the funeral of Manco Capac. The women dance inside a circle of men, who wear long black coats with colored braid and white bone buttons. Trousers are slit down the sides, showing pleated white drawers. The dancers wear a white woolen shawl and long feathers in a head fan.

The Ayarachi dancers go out before dawn to the river where they like to lie on their stomachs and imitate condors washing their feathers. The condors, they say, are their ancestors and the Sun is their god. They kneel and weep when the sun rises over the mountains.

Aimara women, near Juliaca, gaily dressed for the fiesta

Oruro

Frances Toor, in her *Three Worlds of Peru,* describes the week-long dance in Copacabana, Bolivia. This is a town originally laid out "on the blue horizon" by an early Inca as a port for embarking for the sacred Isle of Sacrifices in Lake Titicaca.

A procession goes up to the Calvary on the cone-shaped hill. There beer is sprinkled on the ground for Mother Earth. Professional prayer chanters, with a small Virgin on their heads, bless the dancers in Aimara. Each celebrant leaves a small stone at the foot of the cross. Other chanters bless the people with incense and grant them whatever they wish. Notaries perform pantomime proxy marriage ceremonies, providing the boy or girl with a certificate which is designed to make the marriage come true within a year. People desirous of owning a home and farm animals can buy a miniature house and toy animals and receive a deed: this is to guarantee that their wish will come to pass. Other processions carry images to the lake for them to bless the waters, where celebrants are carried about in white sail boats.

Many dancers perform in the church before the Virgin. For ten *pesos bolivianos,* the priest gives the dancer a lighted candle to be placed before the Virgin. A chorus of boys and girls sings an Aimara hymn. The priest says Mass in Aimara. The celebrants dance out backward from Mary's presence.

As during Inca days in some fiestas, youths playing musical instruments race up an adjacent mountain to a Calvary and return without resting.

Music is almost the same everywhere, though larger places sometimes have modern bands or orchestras. The usual instruments for village gatherings are the flute, mandolin or guitar, and the small harp mounted on a large coffin-shaped sounding board. The drum is also in common use. Other instruments sometimes played are tambourines; the *pincuello,* a horizontal bamboo flute with five or seven openings; accordions, cornets,

A Quiquijana woman in her fiesta costume displays the beauty of native workmanship

A young flute player on the Isla de Sacrificios where Manco Capac lived before founding the great Inca dynasty at Cuzco

chirimitas (a sort of clarinet). The *antara* has twenty to forty bamboo or metal tubes from an inch to fifteen inches long, held by two crossbars—a sort of panpipe, almost like a portable church organ. Itinerant players go from fiesta to fiesta. In the country around Cajamarca, an enormous bamboo trumpet, which has to be held by three helpers, is blown—the roar can be heard for many miles and was probably used in ancient days to transmit messages from mountain to mountain or perhaps in honor of Viracocha, the rising Sun, by the Children of the Sun.

The Moche Fiesta

In Moche on the coast, dances are interspersed with the eating of small crabs and the drinking of toasts from flagons of *chicha*. Each drinker toasts one of the other dancers and tries to empty the flagon at a single draught. The one chosen then toasts another, repeating the ceremony. A popular person or a special visitor is pretty certain to become blind drunk. The dance is a whirling affair in which two dancers approach and retreat and circle each other, waving handkerchiefs.

The dances for Moche's saint, San Isidro, are celebrated the first week in May. The saint is removed from the altar where he is shown working with a pair of oxen and is placed on a table with a green rail around it, holding potted shrubs. Flowers and chains of chiles and paper adorn the platform. San Isidro has a kindly face and wears brown leather breeches, a short red cape, and straw hat turned up in front, adorned with a red and white ribbon. In his right hand, he holds a silver-adorned digging stick, in his left a bag for alms.

The procession carries him under the willow trees along the irrigation banks to various fields. A band leads the way.

The saint spends the night in the house of the owner of the last-visited farm, where he is received with joy and deference. His litter is placed on a household altar hung with colored paper streamers and heaped with local fruits: apples, oranges, figs, lemons, plums. Fireworks are shot off. The host and his friends stay awake all night, enjoying the food, drinks, and dancing. In the morning, the fruit left over is distributed to all the guests.

On May 14 the saint is taken back to the church and the principal procession is made the following day. He is decked out in a silver hat, green velvet cape adorned with gold and precious stones. The table or platform is loaded down with fruit that is later given to the priest.

A devil dance is performed with horned devil masks by

dancers wearing bright-colored trousers, skirts, blouses, and long pink hose. The people dance through the streets to the rhythm made by scraping burro jawbones. That night, being devils, they raid the various orchards with hilarity.

Whenever there is a water shortage, San Isidro is taken to the irrigation ditches. The priest raps on a dike, which is opened to simulate an abundant supply. The witches and the sorcerers sprinkle the fields with seawater to induce the coastal mist that helps conserve the water from the snow mountains. There is never any rain in the area.

Puno

The Puno of Peru, a plateau in the south bordering on Lake Titicaca, in places fifteen thousand feet high, is one of the most beautiful, bleak, and cold regions of the land. In the sunny months, the rocks and many ponds are brightly tinted and the coarse *ichu* grass is green. Wild vicuñas flash over the plain, and large herds of llamas are tended by women in colorful skirts and shawls and by boys in woolen clothing. Here and there the sun glints on deep blue lagoons and on the snow-capped Andes.

In the afternoon the rain pours down. It often turns to hail and ice over which the barefoot Indian women trot unconcernedly, carrying their wares to market in lofty Puno city. Most girls go barefoot, although *cholas,* those of mixed blood, usually wear shoes and wool stockings. Yellow or red skirts are topped by a blue or white blouse and a variegated shawl, fastened perhaps with a jaguar pin with red glass eyes. High-crowned, narrow-brimmed straw hats, or more often felt derbys, complete the costume. Silver earrings dangle beside the brown cheeks.

Puno is a dreary little city of nearly twenty thousand. When the sun is out the walls seem golden and the waters of nearby Lake Titicaca, toward which the streets descend, are blue and

A herder watching his sheep graze on the Puno plateau

gold. Here the Incas, then the Spaniards, came to mine silver and gold as the Aimaras had done before the Incas. The Spaniards built a cathedral on the main Puno plaza. On its facade is carved a mermaid playing a mandolin. Nearly all houses have garden patios with pavements of black and white lake pebbles laid out in designs of birds, animals, and flowers.

Picturesque Julí, a village nearby, has a pleasant plaza with yellow-flowering *culli* trees, a variety of oxalis, and the lake is visible through arches and doorways. The four Jesuit churches are rich with gold, paintings, and saints. The facades are carved Inca style with sun, stars, moon, Indian figures, monkeys, parrots, and flowers.

At the Puno market barter is conducted as in Inca days. When a deal is made, a bit extra is added.

In one market section women are busy at sewing machines, making clothing, from either their own woolen cloth or cloth their customers have woven themselves or purchased. In another corner are restaurants with tables and benches, big *ollas* of stews and soups that are served in glazed terra-cotta bowls.

On sale are the spirited terra-cotta bulls, pigs, and horses made in the village of Santiago. They are filled with *chicha* or *aguardiente* or are banks with a slot in the back.

Most of the herb vendors come in from Bolivia. They wear richer, more colorful clothes than the Peruvians. The women from Amatoria Island are perkily dressed and comb their hair in a dozen small braids on either side. The men wear baggy wool shirts, a poncho or woolen scarf over the shoulders, a woolen cap or derby hat, and sandals. Till about eight years old, boys wear skirts and knitted caps.

Lake Titicaca has been receding for a decade or so, and the large balsas or reed boats with matting sails which previously filled the waters are not seen so often any more; most craft are smaller. Nearly all are made from *totora* reeds tied in bundles at the ends and dried in the sun, then tied together in the desired shape. A place is cut in the front to kneel for paddling. The long

A Chola girl from the beautiful plateau of Puno

Lake Titicaca as seen from the Island of the Sun (Isla de Sacrificios)

paddle is used either kneeling, sitting, or standing. Often the pole is made firm for a sail. The fishnets are made of agave fibers. When the vessel is put in the water, the reeds swell up making it watertight. The making of a new boat is a community enterprise, but the owner provides the food, *chicha,* and music.

The Indians go out in the roughest weather. They cross

Titicaca, big as a sea, fearlessly. On the Pacific coast similar pontoon boats sometimes travel a thousand miles up and down.

On Lake Titicaca on fiesta days people crowd into the balsas and drink and sing all day out on the lake. The musicians usually go along in a separate balsa, playing flutes, mandolins, and harps. Nearly always someone on each boat has a mandolin. During carnival little bags of water with flour sometimes mixed with confetti are hurled from boat to boat making a dreadful mess when they burst.

In the fields, where the carnival is called *pucllay taki*—let us play—the women pull up a few potato plants, wrap them in their shawls, and dance with them. The men toss flowers, coca leaves, and *chicha* to the four points of the compass in honor of Mother Earth. There is music, singing, and gaiety. Half-friendly fights are staged between rival groups. Bare legs are whipped with metal-tipped thongs. The resultant wounds are treated with herbs, mud, saliva, and wine.

Sometimes a tree is transplanted and adorned with flags, ribbons, and gifts: fruits, toys, sandals, baby shoes. It is chopped at by the dancers as they circle it. When it finally topples there is a mad scramble for the gifts.

No people ever created a great society against greater obstacles than did the Quechuas under the leadership of the Incas. No other people in history ever faced and overcame such tremendous geographical and climatic obstacles. They braved the highest and most rugged mountains on earth (except the Himalayas). They conquered heat and snow and learned how to cross chasms thousands of feet deep. They had a more extensive and usable road system than exists in the modern countries. They cultivated the steep sides of enormous slopes, building stone terraces and bringing in water, often by stone aqueducts. A greater area was cultivated than today. Probably no other people in history has utilized a greater share of the technology they possessed. They built great edifices, monuments, and cities. Their arts and sciences were superb. In almost every field of effort they were superior to their conquerors, the Spaniards.

A Quechua family helps us visualize how an Inca family may have looked

Quechua achievements were an astonishment, a great inspiration for all time.

The Conquest shattered the beautifully adjusted timepiece. Their culture was fragmented. The people were largely enslaved in mines and fields. The world swept on past them.

There were a number of great revolts, of course, and the 1816 Independence Congress of Argentina, held in northern Tucumán, seriously considered the restoration of Inca empire with an Incan emperor—a proposal backed by the two most powerful leaders of the revolution.

But the Quechuas have not progressed. Largely still enslaved, they have survived with a stubborn persistence. They are still the major part of the population. Millions still speak the ancient tongues. Their handicrafts still flourish in spite of modern mechanization. Their aesthetic talents have never died. The old roads are gone, and the new ones serve cars and trucks. A few incredible railroads have been built. Airplane fields are found in the highest towns, where takeoff is difficult and often dangerous because of the lofty altitude.

Little by little, the Indians are now recovering the land they lost four centuries ago. The old life follows its serene course in hundreds of remote villages. They still worship the Sun. They are the Children of the Sun. It seems likely that in due time, they will again find their place in the sun. The dream of the old empire still endures.

4 *Ancient Emperors*

Knowing About the Incas

What we know about the ancient Incas comes from the early Spanish historians and the writings of a number of Quechuas who learned the conquerors' language. The Incas themselves had no writing. Everything was recorded in the *quipús,* or knotted cords, which have mostly perished. Some of the chroniclers merit special mention.

Numerous leading Spanish invaders married Virgins of the Sun or girls of the nobility. Chimpu Ocllo, the granddaughter of the Tupac Yupanqui, the tenth Inca, became the common-law wife of Conquistador de la Vega, a knight. Their son, Garcilaso Inca, was born in April 1539 and he achieved fame by his notable reminiscences, and his history of the Incas, *Comentarios Reales,* published in Lisbon in 1609, when he was seventy years old, was the most knowledgeable of the old chroniclers.

His father had gone through several hard campaigns against rebellious Indians and rebellious Spaniards and was rewarded with lands near Cuzco, where he became one of the "eighty manorial lords" of the capital. In Cuzco he put up a palace where he entertained two hundred guests every evening. Extraordinarily wealthy, he had thousands of peasants waiting on him. His wife, Princess Chimpu, bore him two sons.

Young Garcilaso attended bullfights on the estate. Blooded bulls had been brought to Peru almost as soon as horses, sheep, and monks. He was an early bettor at his father's horse races, became an excellent horseman and often went hunting for deer and wild ducks.

In due time Garcilaso went to a school set up for the children of the well-to-do.

The boy was only seven when Gonzalo Pizarro, Francisco's brother, destroyed the forces of the first Spanish viceroy Blasco Núñez Vela, and he saw numerous unruly high-born Spaniards hanged and their heads stuck on posts in the plazà. Among them dangled a lady with her tongue cut out. De la Vega's palace was pillaged before the marauders could be driven off at point-blank range.

Garcilaso's sympathies were with his mother's race. He remembered her as gentle and understanding. Most of her friends were former officials who had been followers of Emperor Huascar, put to death by his half brother Atahualpa. One-time officials and their families often visited her and enjoyed hospitality in the de la Vega palace in Cuzco, where they feasted and drank *chicha* from silver goblets.

Young Garcilaso listened eagerly to the legends of Manco Capac and all the tales of Inca glory and power. He learned the wise sayings of Inca Pachacuti and heard about the great battles of Yupanqui. He learned Indian history, superstitions, and religious beliefs. He loved to sit at the feet of one aged Inca general, who had fought with Inca Huayna Capac and was with him when he died. Garcilaso asked the old man many questions. The general told how the Quechuas began as animals without government or religion, how they were brought together by the Incas and taught the arts of civilization and knowledge of agriculture, and arts and sciences.

Chronicler Polo de Ondegardo showed Garcilaso the mummies of the Incas he had recovered, still wearing the imperial head circlet, their eyes closed with plaques of gold. The boy touched the withered hand of Huayna Capac.

He left for Spain in 1560 at the age of twenty-one and for thirty years fought in the armies of John of Austria and Philip II. Not till 1590, after he settled in Córdoba, did he begin writing the story of his early life, *La Florida del Inca*. He pictured the conquistadors, their courage, vanity, and cruelty. Each was capable of weeping bitterly when his horse died, but slaughtered Quechuas without pity. Most were Don Quixotes but with little kindness or compassion. He contrasted them with the Quechuas, strong and wise, caught in the storm and tragedy of defeat.

His famous *Royal Commentaries of the Incas* is passionately biased in favor of the Incas, though he did not hesitate to tell of their weaknesses, greed, and mistakes. He was more unbiased than most Spanish conquistadors and chroniclers.

Tales of the Chroniclers

Polo de Ondegardo, Cieza de León, and Fernando Montesinos, who crossed the Andes sixty times, were also fierce partisans of the Quechuas. The Jesuit Bernabé Cobo, who was entertained at the de la Vega home, though after Garcilaso had gone to Spain, was intrigued both by Peruvian ladies and the stories of the Inca hierarchy. Juan de Betanzos from Galicia, another soldier who came with Pizarro, settled in Cuzco and married Pizarro's widow, a daughter of Atahualpa, and learned Quechua. He became an official interpreter and negotiator with rebellious Indians in Vilcapampas. His story was finished in 1557, but only a portion of it was finally published in 1880.

Except for several scribes put to work by Viceroy Francisco de Toledo, few of the Spanish chroniclers sympathized with the conquerors. The best of Toledo's writers was Pedro Sarmiento de Gamboa, a sailor. He checked out his story with fifty-two surviving Inca nobles; hence his book contains much authentic historical material. However, his work was not published until 1906.

Pedro de Cieza de León, born in Estremadura, had come to America as a sailor when only fourteen, first serving in Cartagena, but a few years later was part of Valdivia's terrible expedition to the Cauca valley in Columbia. He was a witness to the savagery of the conquest, but was humane and sympathetic toward the native people, besides being an accurate observer. He started his chronicle in Cauca valley in 1541, telling about the "great and strange things" of the New World, what he had observed with his own eyes, and what he had learned from "persons of good repute." While his companions slept, he wore himself out writing. "Neither fatigue nor the ruggedness of the country, nor the mountains and rivers, nor hunger and suffering, have ever been able to obstruct my two duties, namely writing and following my flag and my captain."

He traveled to Quito, Ecuador, and all over Peru, finally becoming a *corregidor,* a Crown official, in Cuzco. He was thirty two in 1650 when he finished the first part of his *Crónica de Peru,* a travel story in which he described Inca roads and bridges. His next volume described the Incan system of government and the history of the various rulers. Along with Polo and Garcilaso he wrote one of the great classics of early colonial literature.

From such authorities, we are able to piece together the way of life under the Incas.

Meet the Incas

Inca Lloque Yupanqui, the third Inca, started to extend and consolidate the boundaries of his realm very soon after his father Sinchi Roca, the second Inca, son of Manco Capac, the founder, died.

Yupanqui was called the "Left-Handed Man on Whose Qualities You Can Depend." Indian chronicler Huamán Poma describes him as ugly, with a protuberance on his nose, eyes too large, a narrow mouth, with two broken teeth. He attired himself in true royal fashion in a crimson turban and tunic, three handsome belts, and sandals, and usually presented himself in public with a lance and shield.

Poma also described the Inca's wife, Coya Mama Cahua, as equally unattractive, a moody person who wept without cause, avoided other women, had no interest in people, and was often drunk. She had little concern for her household and mostly ate raw food. But she bore the Inca many children.

In planning conquest, he defended his southern flank by building a fortress to keep the not-yet-conquered Aimaras at bay, while he consolidated the central region around Cuzco. At the beginning of the thirteenth century, he moved past Lake Titicaca to conquer the people in what is now Bolivia.

His son, Mayta Capac, the fourth Inca, continued the conquest. He was a pale, loosely boned, melancholy man of great courage. Very fond of his wife, he had numerous children by her, of whom two, Apu Maytas and Balcac, became successful military leaders in the final conquest of the Aimaras and the Collas of Bolivia.

By crossing the Cordillera Real (fifteen to eighteen thousand feet), the Inca's forces reached Tiahuanaco, the mighty ruins that filled them with admiration and awe. The high Bolivian plain, often dry, desolate, and frozen, lay before the invaders. Their soothsayers interpreted a flaming meteor as a promise the enemy would be conquered.

The first great battle occurred near the Huchuy River—a day-long, hand-to-hand fight. The bronze clubs of the Aimaras broke more than half a thousand Quechua heads, but they themselves lost six thousand men. They were surrounded, and at dawn Mayta Capac appeared in his golden litter and sent messages offering peace. The bloodied enemy chiefs knelt before him, ropes around their necks.

Travelers contemplate the long walk ahead of them on the Bolivian plateau

He ordered them freed, saying, as such conquerors always say, "I have come to teach you and enrich you. Worship our god and obey our orders for your own good." The Incas rarely carried out vengeance as policy of war or peace; they tried, however, to implant their own culture and systems, which in most cases were patently superior. Mayta Capac told his men, according to chronicler Pedro Sarmiento de Gambóa, "Spare the enemy and his dwellings; soon they will be ours." One of the Inca's first orders was to take a census of the region.

The Incas were interested in the bronze weapons of the Collas, and were astonished by the smelter furnaces that flared red in the dusk on Mount Potosí above the great silver city of the same name, on the surrounding heights.

"There were so many [Aimara] furnaces in Potosí," wrote chronicler Bernabé Cobo, "that the mountain was illuminated." Men were boldly silhouetted as they fed the hearths with dry shrubs or llama dung. The furnaces were of baked earth, perforated for a draft, filled with ore crushed by heavy blocks of granite. An earth stone crusher was handled by four men. Thousands of workers dried the ore, transported it, crushed it, tended the fires, and carried the refined metal to workshops.

Bolivia was a great addition for the Quechuas, for they gained most of their knowledge of mining, refining, and working metals from the Colla or Aimara people, though not until the fifth Inca, Capac Yupanqui, did the Inca seriously attempt to take over the mines. He assembled the greatest army yet created, well trained and well armed. Near Potosí he won over the enemies by arbitrating the differences between two rival chieftains and persuading them to accept the rule and law of the empire. "The Sun [with whom the hero identified himself] assures peace and prosperity to all his children," he told them. He distributed vicuña wool garments, jewels set in gold, and personally escorted the enemy leaders to their homes.

Thus Potosí, the richest prize of the continent, was finally secured without the loss of a single man. The Incas inherited the Aimaras' advanced knowledge of metallurgy.

Under them artisanship was improved. They produced gold and silver weapons, bracelets, necklaces, leg ornaments, crowns, belts, mirrors, and cups and manufactured hair tweezers and other instruments, such as surgical tools for trepanning the skull and performing brain operations.

Potosí was a sugar-loaf mountain, rising a mile above the plain—that is, four miles above sea level—and was often covered with snow. It and the region about had enormous deposits of silver, tin, gold, and lead. Mercury was used to refine silver, and the Aimaras had already learned how to alloy tin and copper.

Aimara women from Bolivia dressed in their traditional woolen shawls

Later, under the Spaniards, Potosí became the greatest silver center in the world. A city of 200,000, larger than any in Spain, sprang up in that bleak, cold region. The metal was then transported, not to Cuzco, but to the coast, to be taken to Spain.

The Incas had previously exported metallurgical objects. Spanish pilot Bartolomeo Ruiz met a raft from the Gulf of Guayaquil—this was before Pizarro's conquest of Peru—and described the elaborate gold and silver objects being transported, probably to Mexico. Even at a more remote time, such trade existed. An American scholar has discovered two gold discs in Guatemala which had come from the earlier Chavín civilization.

Capac Yupanqui next sent his eldest son by his second wife, tall handsome Roca (already designated heir to the throne), with forces to bring the nearest coast peoples, the Nazca kingdom, under his domain. He was instructed to bring back a number of Nazca families to be settled in the Apurimac Valley. Roca easily persuaded most of the region, for nearly 500 miles along the shore, to accept Cuzco rule. From the hill peoples he first subdued he learned to chew coca and how to use fish meal as fertilizer.

The Kidnapped Prince

Inca Roca married Micay, the beautiful daughter of the chief of neighboring Huayllacán. She bore him four sons: Cusi Hualpa, the prince regent; Paucar, a warrior; Huamán; and Vicaquirú, who became a famous general.

The marriage brought strife to the kingdom. Beautiful Micay had been promised to Tocay Capac, chief of the Aymaracas, a powerful people just beyond the fertile valley where the Huayllacas lived, some twenty miles from Cuzco. The Aymaraca chief considered this a rank betrayal and went to war

It is easy to imagine the wealth and the dignity of the Incas amid the surroundings of Lake Titicaca

with the Huayllacas. The latter, less numerous, resisted valiantly and only after many years did they sue for peace, which the Aymaraca chief granted, with the secret proviso that the Inca's oldest son, Cusi Hualpa, then a boy of eight, be delivered to him. Otherwise the Huayllacas would be completely exterminated.

The Huayllaca chief was deeply upset, caught between terrible alternatives. He had no wish to see his grandson in the power of the Aymaraca chief but had no other recourse than to comply. Not could he offend the Inca, for the penalty would be more terrible than that threatened by the Aymaracas. A plot was cooked up by which he could avoid being blamed.

He asked the Inca that the prince, his grandson, be allowed to visit his mother's relatives. The Inca considered this a reasonable request and sent the boy with a retinue of twenty attendants to the palace in Paulú, the chief town of the Huayllacas.

He was received with great fiestas befitting his rank. As it was hot summertime, the boy watched the celebration from the shade of a flower-decked trellis.

Presently, everybody was ordered out to the harvest field, leaving the prince lolling on the trellised veranda. The entire town, old and young, boys and girls, went out with their tools, singing the harvest song, until their voices faded in the distance.

The boy played among the flowers, completely alone except for his attendants. Without warning, the war cry *Atau! Atau!* was heard on all sides. His attendants, all *orejones*—big-ear nobles—fought valiantly to protect him, but all were killed, and the prince was abducted.

The raiders brought the child into the presence of Tocay Capac in his chief abode, The Place of Warp and Woof, shouting, "Behold the prisoner we have brought with us!"

"Is this the child of Mama Micay, who should have been my wife?"

The prince himself answered, "I am the son of the great Inca Roca and the Queen Mama Micay."

Tocay Capac gleamed with satisfaction and ordered the prince taken out and killed.

The prince stood up straight and cried out scornfully, "I warn you that if you murder me, a curse will fall upon you and your children. All will be wiped out, and not even a memory of you and your people will be left."

Tears of blood flowed from his eyes.

"He weeps blood!" everybody shouted, amazed and horrified. Filled with fear, they shrank back to keep from touching him. Even the chief was shaken by the mystery of blood and feared the boy's curse. Not daring again to order his followers to kill him, he had the boy handed over to shepherds of llama herds on the heights overlooking the great plain. The climate there was very harsh and they were ordered to reduce his food each day until he died.

But the shepherds liked the boy, who was friendly and helpful, and did not starve him. The winter was very terrible, but the prince seemed to grow stronger with the exposure. They kept him hidden there for a year.

Meanwhile the Huayllaca chief expressed great sorrow over the kidnapping. He informed Inca Roca that the most diligent efforts were still being made to discover the criminals. He was doing everything possible. Inca Roca was suspicious but dared not attack or make any hostile move, lest the prince, if still alive, be killed. As the months went by, he despaired of ever seeing him again.

One of Tocay Capac's concubines, Chimpu Irma, a daughter of the chief of the Antas near Cuzco, had witnessed the scene at court when the boy had wept blood and had heard the order that he be sent to live with the shepherds. Her heart was troubled, but not until she visited her family in Anta did she dare do anything. She made inquiries and was able to arrange

that the shepherds and guards allow Cusi Hualpa to join in a
fiesta in which the boys raced to the top of a hill near the
shepherds' huts. Such races were common among the young
males of the realm, for the fastest runners would be chosen as
chasquis, or king's messengers, who enjoyed many privileges.

Chimpu Irma's friends in Anta waited, well armed, just
beyond the summit of the hill. The prince outdistanced all the
other boys and was easily taken off by his rescuers.

They were pursued by the Aymaraca guards, who overtook
them on the banks of a small lake—Huaylla Puna. The guards
were defeated, and the men of Anta brought their prize into
their chief town, a small place on the side of a hill overlooking
the vast plain of Suriti. There the rescued prince was received
with great rejoicing. Chimpu Irma held him close with tears of
gladness.

But the Antas had to be very discreet and hid him out, not
sending word to the Inca. Not for a year more did they feel it
was safe to let Roca know.

The Inca questioned the Anta messengers in person, unable
to believe his son was still alive. The news seemed too good to
be true. He sent a secret emissary, disguised as a mendicant, to
Anta to find out the truth. This man brought back word that
the prince was alive at Anta.

At once the chief lords of Cuzco were dispatched with rich
presents of gold, silver, and jewels to the Anta chief, asking that
the Inca's son be sent home. The Anta chief replied that the boy
had so won the hearts of his people that they did not wish to
lose him, but he had to agree that the boy should return to his
father. He declined the presents and requested instead that he
and his followers be accepted as relatives of the Inca and be
honored as *orejones,* and made part of the Peruvian nobility.

Roca agreed. After the prince was restored to his arms, the
emperor journeyed to Anta and there publicly declared that all
prominent Antas would henceforth be considered *orejones.*
Doubtless some painful ear splitting and stretching followed.

Roca learned how the Huayllacas had been careless in

guarding the boy and was inclined to punish them. But they begged for mercy, and Cusi Hualpa also asked that they be forgiven for they had treated him royally. Reluctantly Inca Roca pardoned them. Tocay Capac died about this time, and so the Aymaracas escaped the long-delayed punishment that Roca had sworn to impose on them.

Roca had had a long glorious reign expanding the empire and organizing it on the basis of equality and justice. He sent Captain Apo Camor, the Tiger, with ten thousand men to invade the eastern jungles, the headwaters of the Amazon. The expedition went down the Paucartambo River in balsas to Chuncho Indian country, a region of dense almost impenetrable vegetation, where the soldiers suffered from insects, hunger, and thirst. They ate up most of the parrots they came upon, then were reduced to eating roots and wild fruit. The Tiger rested on a hammock with a plump Chuncho girl and sent his troops home with parrots and caged animals for the royal zoo. The soldiers were received as heroes in the Cuzco plaza.

After various imperial expeditions into the Amazon area, tropical products showed up in Cuzco; much-prized *chonta,* the tough palm tree wood, new medicinal herbs, bird feathers, resins, manioc, fruits such as the *chirimoya,* mango, avocado, coconuts. The all-powerful monarch enjoyed more luxuries.

Eyes Weeping Blood

Prince Cusi Hualpa took the name Yahuar Huaccac, Weeping Blood. He ascended the throne and proved to be a wise firm ruler, interested chiefly in the welfare of his people. With the aid of his brother, General Vicaquirú, and his uncle, General Apu Maytas, he extended the boundaries of the realm still further. New tribes were incorporated into the empire, and the Inca system was imposed on them, with all its privileges and its greater technical know-how.

Yahuar Huaccac had five sons by a wife chiefly interested

in tame parrots and trained monkeys. As a youth, his eldest son Viracocha aroused his father's displeasure. He was quarrelsome and wild and contemptuous of religion. He broke idols and tried to set fire to the temples. As punishment he was sent to guard the llama herd of the Sun in the Chiuta pasture, well outside of Cuzco. Years later he returned without permission and demanded to see his father at the holy midday hour of silent worship. The Inca flew into a rage and sent out word he would be put to death.

Viracocha forced his way into the royal apartments. He told his father that a strange, aged visitor, who claimed to be a brother of the first Incas, had warned him of revolt brewing in the northern provinces.

"You are mad," his father answered. "Go and tend your llamas."

Several months later the Chanca, Vilca, and Huamarca people raised an army of thirty thousand and revolted. The Inca fled from Cuzco.

His son appeared again and upbraided his father for abandoning his palace. Determined to defeat the rebel forces, he gathered four thousand volunteers. A call was sent out to all faithful Quechuas and Aimaras, and the prince soon had twenty thousand men. He advanced to the hills and plain outside the capital to give battle.

The trumpets blew and the bronze missiles were hurled. All day the struggle surged to and fro. Toward the close of the afternoon, the Chanca's right wing was thrown back, and a contingent of five thousand Quechua soldiers, whom Viracocha had concealed on a hill, surged down and overwhelmed them. Thirty thousand dead covered the plain.

The prince led his troops back to the capital, striding at their head, covered with dust and blood. The people threw down fruit and flowers and sang songs of joy,

His mother the queen greeted him in the Joy Plaza and led him to the Temple of the Sun. He took off his shoes at the door, and the priests sacrificed a white llama.

He took over the empire from his senile father, started to fortify Sacsahuamán and built a new elaborate temple to sun-god Viracocha, whose name he bore, about fifty miles from Cuzco. He led Inca forces into Argentina and Chile. The invaders were admitted peacefully to the Diaguitas fortresses. They marveled at the fine pottery and well-tilled fields and curious customs, such as the rites of the rainmakers and the planting of arrows about a sick person.

Viracocha ordered a new canal built for them. Supplied by cold mountain lakes, it was nine feet wide by twelve feet deep and 300 miles long. It was cut through stone mountains and then crossed the desert.

Pachacutec

The ninth Inca, Pachacutec, tall and lion-eyed, interested himself in education. Surrounded by the professors, priests, and army officers, he personally presented the ornate diplomas of *Yacha Huasi,* the great university, and addressed the graduates. He sent schoolmasters throughout the provinces to spread the Quechua language and settled whole families among newly conquered provinces to teach them the arts and crafts.

A fervent moralistic reformer, he instituted a regime of strict austerity for his subjects, high and low, and he sought to stem debauchery and curb luxurious living. He preached against rage which denoted a weak character, and jealousy, for it distilled its poisons from the brain and tissues "like a spider from the most beautiful flowers."

Punishment for the five cardinal wrongdoings: lying, laziness, theft, murder, and debauchery, was made more severe. Theft from the king was punished by the prisoner being flung into a ravine or strung up by the heels till dead; theft from priests was punished by being beaten to death. Cowards, too, he decreed, should be hanged, for otherwise they would become thieves. He reformed the judicial system. Judges who accepted

gifts were to be punished as thieves. Trials had to respect the rights of the accused, though neither women nor the poor, who were too easily misled, were allowed to be witnesses.

He pulled down much of Cuzco and rebuilt it along palatial lines, an ambitious program of urban renewal. The Temple of the Sun was enlarged. The newer building blocks were smaller regular square or rectangular stones perfectly fitted and mostly polished, providing more tailored and uniform, if less dramatic, walls.

The rushing waters of the Watay, the larger stream flowing through the city, were covered over with great stone slabs, and a permanent water supply was brought in by underground conduits. He improved the central plazas and pushed the work on Sacsahuamán, where he went nearly every day in his litter to watch the thousands of toiling workmen moving stones—often nine feet high and weighing as much as ten tons—into place. He finished the walls facing the town and the outer enclosures of the other side. Two portals, the Gateway of Sand and the Gateway of Achuana (name of the architect) provided access. A third entrance, the Gateway of Viracocha, would eventually be added in a third wall.

His brother was leading new armies to the north, steadily pushing out the frontiers. He took the emperor's son, sixteen-year-old Tupac Yupanqui, with him to conquer the rich land of Cajamarca and the northern coast. Fifty thousand men were led forth and reached northern Huayllas region, the site of ancient Chavín.

The subduing of Cajamarca took four months of hard fighting. At one time his twelve-hundred -mile line of communication was threatened. The force returned finally to Cuzco in triumph. The emperor set to work at once to appoint local officials, build roads, and direct the establishment of new industries. It took three years to consolidate the new territory.

A new army of forty thousand men was outfitted to march over the northern coastal areas. It took nearly a year to subdue

A cross in a town square decorated for a religious festival

them. The prince of Huaraz offered strong resistance. All the communities to the north of the Rimac River were overrun, including the great Chimú city and its temples, later to become Trujillo.

Next, Tupac Yupanqui, taking charge of the army in person, pushed the conquest on into Ecuador and southern Colombia, then through the Andes to the Pacific to overpower the Chonos. To take Guayaquil, he had to build a fleet of canoes and train his men to handle them. He camped finally on the site for a year, before attempting to conquer Puna Island in the river.

Moving south to Tumbes, where the Spaniards later landed, traders brought goods on huge balsa rafts with sails. They told him they were from the Fire Islands far out to sea, today known as the Galápagos Islands. His necromancer authenticated the tales, and he proceeded to have built a great number of balsas, made from inflated seal intestines, and rafts made from logs covered with cane matting, each large enough for a small thatched cabin. He loaded twenty thousand of his men aboard, and vanished over the horizon. Nearly a year later he returned with a "black" Indian princess, gold, a brass chair, and a large shell, probably from a great tortoise, the species at which Darwin later marvelled and from which he got the clue for his great theory of the *Origin of the Species.*

On his father's death in 1492, the year of Columbus's discovery of America, the crown prince took over, calling himself Inca Huayna Capac, the "Young Chief Rich in Virtues."

Revolt soon broke out. He was in the south and hastened to Cuzco, according to chronicler Cieza de León. He whipped together an army of 200,000 warriors and set forth attended by *yanacones* and camp women. He took along his own household of 2,000 women. All rebellion was quickly put down, and he went on to Ecuador.

On a previous trip to Quito he had taken as one of his wives, beautiful Tocto Coca, daughter of the deposed king of Quito. Eventually she would have become queen of the Ecuadorean realm. She gave him a son, Atahualpa. The Inca loved Quito and Tocto Coca and his handsome son, and this time he never went back to Cuzco, where he had left another wife.

Quito, located in a rich densely populated region, was, after Cuzco, the most splendid city of the empire. He settled down in a fine country palace to enjoy life with Tocto Coca and in due time Atahualpa took charge of northern affairs.

One day he sent for his legitimate younger son Huascar, born of his wife, Rahua Ocllo in Cuzco, and informed him he was dividing the empire into a northern kingdom, Ecuador, to be ruled by Atahualpa, the rest to be ruled from Cuzco by Huascar. After his death, the two half-brothers quarreled, went to war, and Huascar was executed. But this was at the end of the empire. The Spaniards were at the door.

Court Life

Chronicler Garcilaso gave a vivid description of court life. The Inca sat on a throne of solid gold, without arms or back, but with a concave seat, placed on a great square slab of gold. All the cups for the entire service of the palace, for the table or for the kitchen, large and small, were of gold and silver, and some were placed in each inn on the highway for the use of the emperor when he traveled, so as to avoid the necessity of carrying them when journeying in the provinces. There was also a great store of new clothing, both for wearing and for the bed. The Inca never put on the same dress twice, but after wearing it gave it to his relatives. All bedclothes were woven from the wool of the vicuña. The Incas did not have mattresses.

"Dinner was abundant, ample for all the Inca's relatives, who might come to dine, and for the numerous servants. The principal meal, for the Inca as for all the people, was at eight or nine in the morning. They supped before sundown. . . . These two meals were the only ones. Even though they ate little, they were not so abstemious [when indulging in their after-meals] drinking. . . . They went to bed early, and got up very early to do the day's business."

The Incas, however, ate foods little used by the commoners, such as fresh fish and meat. Special delicate native tubers such as *yuchic* and *cuchuchú* were served.

Travelers from Puno take a break for lunch

The palace—and each emperor usually built a new one for his own use—was enormous, with patios, gardens, halls, apartments. Instead of tapestries, the walls were covered with gold or silver. The women used bronze mirrors, but the *ñustas* (holy virgins), the *coya* (queen), and the ladies of the nobility preened themselves before finely made mirrors of obsidian, a natural glass, or of pyrite or silver. The *coya* had many maids who took care of her person, bathed her, washed her hair, trimmed her nails, applied cosmetics, and dressed her.

Servants were innumerable. Sweepers wielded their twig brooms, water carriers brought in fresh water, porters brought supplies, woodcutters provided fuel. There were keepers of the wardrobe, treasury guards, gardeners, domestics for every task. Courtiers served meals, though in the palace this duty was performed by the Inca's concubines. Each particular service was carried on by natives of particular villages, obliged to supply the necessary personnel—a form of tribute. The villagers rotated in the service, and the community was responsible for their good conduct and efficiency. If any servant committed a serious offense against the Incas, the village was razed.

Once every three years great hunts were carried out. The main hunt was observed by the Inca from a richly adorned tent. Ten thousand to sixty thousand men fanned out in a great circle which was gradually reduced as beaters drove the game ahead with shouts and a great din. When the creatures had been corralled, trained slayers moved in on them with three-stone bolas, clubs, and sticks. Deer, pumas, bears, foxes, wildcats were slaughtered. Female animals were rarely killed.

The wild vicuñas yielded the finest fur known in the kingdom, all of which went to the Inca. The coarse *guanaco* wool went to the hunters, who also received venison, skins, hides, and feathers. Every province had four hunting areas each of which was utilized in turn once a year.

Inca funerals were celebrated with great pomp and rich trappings. The embalmed body was sumptuously attired and kept on the throne attended by a staff of servants even after death. In earlier days friends and relatives killed themselves in sorrow, but in later years, fealty was satisfied by sacrificing llamas named after the relatives. Royal mummies were brought out in public on special occasions.

Old Ways and Holy Days 5

The Empire of the Sun

More than armed conquest, the Inca expansion was a process of economic, political, and cultural amalgamation. Over the centuries an adequate administration was developed. Each emperor made his contributions, good and evil.

Conquered towns and tribal *ayllus* (clans) were rarely punished. Frequently their chiefs were invited to the palace in Cuzco—a generosity continued throughout the entire period of the empire—and their sons were educated there.

The chief concern was to promote agriculture and to provide revenues for the Crown. Under this system the *ayllus* became less and less based on blood kinship, but increasingly on the soil they tilled. They were divided into groups of ten husbandmen, each headed by a *chunca camayoc*. A *pachaca chunca camayoc* headed up ten groups. Other officials headed fifty, five hundred, one thousand, and ten thousand. The *hunu camayoc,* the chief of ten thousand, was a member of the royal family, with large gold discs in his distended ears.

Dressed in turban and cloak he visited newly conquered

areas and brought word to them that the land belonged not to
man but to God, to Viracocha, the Sun.

The land was divided into three parts, and each family head
received a *tupú,* a lot large enough for the sowing of a hundred
pounds of corn. Each son received an additional *tupú,* each
daughter a half-*tupú.* Thus the larger the family became, the
more land it cultivated.

One third of the common land was set aside for communal
cultivation, a third for the emperor and the officials, and the
priests of the sun cult. The crops of another third went to
support soldiers, invalids, the aged, and orphans.

Specialists determined which crop was most suitable and
the best manner of irrigating it. The authorities provided the
necessary fertilizer that was not obtained by organic farming,
such as llama manure or, in later days, fish from the sea, and
guano—bird droppings—from the islands. Granaries, established by the first Inca, were widely extended, so the commis-
sary was able to provide food rations in January, or midsum-
mer, before the crops could be harvested. Elaborate irrigation
works were carried out.

From time to time a regular official, the *totrioc michoc,*
inspected the villages and the workers. These officials were
trained from birth to control the provinces, to settle all land
disputes and to mete out rewards and punishments. They were
celibates of a special caste, who always had their ear lobes split
so they hung down their cheeks in two strips. Royal treasurers
also appeared with *quipús* to record the number of people and
their possessions, the land areas, and the amount of the crop.

The male and female population were each divided into ten
groups. The warriors included all males from twenty to fifty.
Those from fifty to eighty years became servants of noblemen,
with light duties. Old men over eighty, mostly able only to eat
and sleep, planted roses and cared for the domesticated *cuyes*
and ducks. The fourth group was made up of the sick, deaf,
dumb, and blind, hunchbacked, dwarfed, and mutilated, who
gave what service they could. Males from eighteen to twenty

carried messages and tended herds. They practiced poverty and abstinence and were forbidden to marry. Those from twelve to eighteen tended herds, hunted birds, and gave the feathers to the chief. Boys from nine to twelve protected small birds, the plants, and harvests from other birds and animals. Those from five to nine years, called top-spinners, were carefully trained and were punished for bad conduct. Parents were allowed to care for, protect, and enjoy children up to five. Infants in the cradle made up the tenth group.

Women were put in similar groups. The warrior's wife did the spinning, weaving, and making of clothes. Widows wove and cooked. The older women tended children. The fourth group, cripples and dwarfs, the blind, the deaf, and dumb, could marry only their own kind. The *cipasconas* were girls ripe for marriage, the upper limit being thirty years. The prettiest, before twenty, were chosen to go to Cuzco or other centers as *ñustas,* where they might become wives or concubines of the Inca nobles, high officials, chiefs, and warriors. Theoretically no one could choose a wife according to his own wishes. For important personages marriage had to be sanctioned by the Inca; for lesser citizens, by the proper local official.

The "Shavelings," girls from nine to twelve, wore short skirts and went barefoot. They learned to cook and spin and prepared *chicha.* All girls of this age were depilated—that is, all their body hair was removed. "Little girls" gathered flowers and helped their parents. Still younger ones could play, but had to look after their younger brothers and sisters and fetch water from wells for cooking. Next came those learning to walk; finally, infants.

This amazing, somewhat rigid system was applied successfully to millions of human beings. Justice and the elimination of poverty kept people contented. Ruling so many people over such vast areas was made possible by good communications, good organization, common religion, inculcated patriotism, and the training of thousands of *quipú* keepers, who kept the records.

Knotted Cords

Various knotted cords represented different types of *quipús*. That of the Inca, thick and black, had a main cord to which were attached many multicolored smaller cords for any calculations or records—household servants, the llama herds, the storehouses, the crop yields, the gold and silver supply. In the middle of the main cord was a big knot to which was attached a heavy red cord. Each knot in the red cord represented a year of the Inca's reign. Numerous lesser cords were attached to the knots to record the number of conquered provinces. Green threads were knotted to indicate the battles, the enemies killed, the number of royal troops killed, the booty obtained, the population absorbed, the probable production, and other important matters.

Additional records were kept by painting cloth, pottery, gourds, and boards that resembled plywood. Viceroy Toledo examined fabrics that depicted the Incas and their wives, the creation of the world by Viracocha, historical events, and battles. Many such records were found deposited in the royal Inca archives.

Roads and Bridges

The Inca roads as engineering feats were greater than those of Rome. They ran along the mountainsides for fifteen hundred miles north from Cuzco, and a thousand miles south to Chile, Bolivia, and Argentina. Another main road ran along the coast from Chile to northern Peru. Lateral roads ran down to the coast and to the Amazon jungles. In places, upland roads— perhaps to control snow—were lined with stone walls. Desert roads were often lined with adobe walls to keep off drifting sands. In places, the upper-level roads became carved stone

An ancient tambo *or inn situated beside an Inca road*

steps, easily negotiated by *chasquis,* foot travelers, llamas—but not horses.

Suspension bridges carried them over mighty canyons. These bridges were suspended from stone towers on either bank, by thick agave fiber cables, across which slats were laid. Smaller cables provided railings or hand supports.

Some of these bridges or their towers are still in existence, sometimes still in use. If he likes your smile, the conductor on the train from Cuzco down the Urubamba gorge under great Andean snow giants to Machu Picchu, the world's most spectacular ruins, will signal the engineer to halt and wait while you photograph a bridge over the rushing river. It consists of two Inca-built shore towers and a massive Inca pier in the center of the stream, but the old fiber cables have been replaced with iron beams and steel ropes.

At convenient intervals on the roads were wayside inns for travelers and the *chasquis* who ran in fast relays from Colombia to Argentina on official missions. The relays covered nearly two hundred miles a day. Fish was brought from the coast in about a day. These inns had food stored in stone bins, and the supply was so ample that the Spaniards lived off them for years.

Like the earlier men of Chavín, the Quechuas were remarkable stoneworkers. They seem to have been able to carve granite as though it were chalk. One of the techniques was to bore a hole in stone, fill it with water, then seal it up tight. When the water froze in winter, the stone was split apart. In such ways they built massive stone aqueducts that irrigated lofty terraced fields.

Sometimes they bored through stone mountains to bring in water. Such inner mountain conduits brought water to lofty Machu Picchu, where it flowed through a series of bath rooms, each with its tub hewn out of the stone slope in singularly modern style. These still exist. They have angled corners; each has a seat at one end, stone hand bars, and indentations to hold ointments, perfumes, and cosmetics.

Farm and Village Life

There on the steep slopes of Machu Picchu, as everywhere in the highlands, the Incas built terraces filled in with loam for their crops and orchards. They grew cherries, plums, and peaches. They planted their chief staff of life—potatoes—more than a hundred varieties of assorted shapes and colors; beans, corn, *oca*, chile, *quinóa*, quinine, coca, cotton trees, agave, and false-pepper trees. They conserved their potatoes by freezing or dehydration, shrinking them to hard black marbles. Ground up, they made a *chunno* flour for gruel.

In northern central Peru a Quechua peasant, his wife, and five children—two boys, three girls—lived in a stone thatched-roof house of three rooms, without windows, with inner niches for cupboards. It was set in a corn and potato field, and as in other villages, the farmer also had access to the forested communal lands. Part of the lands were cultivated by all the villagers for charity purposes, another for the Inca. The harvests were turned over to the Inca treasurer who recorded them on *quipús* that were sent to Cuzco. A share of the crop was sent to sustain the imperial household, which in turn contributed to needy communities. It was used to support the army, the royal llama herdsmen, and artisans. Part went to the storage bins of the inns. Another portion was allotted to the priests. A portion went to the local governing *sinchi* or *curaca* and lesser officials.

In return for this effort the villager was supplied with llama meat from the royal herds, sometimes venison, either fresh or as *charqui,* that is, dried meat.

The family meal usually consisted of a soup with meat, boiled or roasted corn, roasted or boiled potatoes or, occasionally, potato gruel made from *chuño* seasoned with red pepper,

A Quechua mother with her child

salt, and other herbs and spices. This is still a favorite soup throughout the highlands. Other soups were made from *oca* roots or *quinóa*. Corn, or *sara*, bread was hard for the ordinary use, or soft and fine for special occasions or religious ceremonies. Cooking was done in clay or stone ovens, with openings for draft, and in homemade or bought utensils of clay or stone. Beautifully carved wooden or gourd dishes and spoons were used. After meals they drank homemade beer made from corn, false-pepper berries, peanuts, maguey leaves, or any fruit.

Coca-leaf chewing was a royal monopoly, not universal as it later became. *Sayri,* or tobacco, was used only for snuff to clear the nasal passages.

The peasant wore a loincloth, a shirt, a cape, and sandals, a felt hat or woolen cap, and he had a leather or fiber pouch. His head was wrapped in a fillet, and he had adornments such

Women gossiping in the bread store

as arm bracelets and brooches. His wife wore a long tunic, a cape, a felt hat, sandals, brooches, bracelets, necklaces, and other ornaments.

Clothing was made from woolen yarn provided from the royal herds or cotton brought from the coast. But each couple, on getting married, received from the Inca two outfits, everyday attire and a fiesta dress. The wool was spun on a hand spindle, and the yarn was woven in primitive looms into cloth, shawls, blankets, ponchos, and rugs.

Each community had its special market day three times a month, though some vendors were there every day. Large centers had very elaborate markets. Great regional fairs were held. To the more famous ones people came from hundreds of miles, to celebrate some religious event.

Town or provincial meetings were called at the markets on holidays, and there new laws or edicts were announced.

Goods on the market were not sold for gold or silver, which had no monetary significance, but mostly by barter, though corn or maize was often used as money. The trading, except for a few products such as *cuyes*, birds, animals, and tools—hoes, axes, adzes, rakes, knives—was done by the women.

The chronicler Bernabé Cobo described the method. The women placed their merchandise—corn, potatoes, beans, fruit—in little piles in even rows. The buyer sat down near the seller and made a small heap of maize which she considered sufficient to purchase, say a pile of peanuts or coca roots. The seller paid no attention, and the buyer reluctantly added a kernel or two of corn. No words were spoken. If the seller was too greedy, the buyer would go elsewhere. But when the seller considered the payment sufficient, she gathered up the corn and handed over what the buyer sought.

Getting Married

The nobles had many wives. Later wives were subservient to the first wife. On her death, he chose a new first wife—

usually a girl not of his household—though a period of two to three years of mourning had to be observed. The ordinary Quechua usually had only one wife.

In some villages the local official periodically assembled those of marriageable age, paired them off, and married them. In other places, the boy went to the girl's parents with a present —perhaps a bagful of coca leaves. If accepted he then did household chores, carrying wood or working in the field for several days, while the relatives dickered over the proper gifts to be given for the girl. On the marriage day she was formally presented to the groom in the presence of the kinfolk of both. He knelt and shod her right foot with a woolen sandal or, if she was a widow, with a grass-woven sandal. After the ceremony he led her to their new house, already built by both families. The bride took from her girdle a fine woolen shirt for her husband, a fillet to bind his hair, and a breast ornament, which he put on at once.

They were then separated, and each spent the remainder of the day with elder persons of the same sex who advised them on the duties and obligations of matrimony. Many gifts were presented and well before nightfall a fiesta got under way, with much *chicha,* music, and dancing. This process and ceremony are present in many villages to this day.

The Inca's Visit

A great day came for the villager and his family when he was personally visited by the Inca. The ruler made frequent trips to all parts of the empire, a habit particularly of the seventh ruler, Yahuar Huaccac, who had great concern for the poor. His first major trip to the interior followed a dreadful epidemic. He wished to reassure the people and pray to the local gods.

The peasant was astonished one day to see the yellow-clad Cañaris guards of the emperor approaching his house. The

Cañaris of northern Peru had fought an earlier Inca more fiercely than any other people. When they were finally subdued, he commended them for their bravery and declared that thereafter the royal guards would always be Cañaris.

They lined up before the humble dwelling. Royal palm bearers swept the ground and strewed flowers. The royal litter appeared, richly adorned. The top was covered with palm leaves, and colored tassels dangled from the lower edges. Golden objects hung inside, and the sides and seats were covered with rich vicuña cloth. The high sides had an opening, screened when traveling, to permit easy entering or leaving. The king rode backward facing the queen.

The Inca was wearing his royal fillet and tall red plumes, his fine cape and richly decorated shirt, and vicuña sandals with fur inside. The queen's shawl was held by a large silver brooch, and her headdress of finest crimson cloth flowed from her crown down her back.

The litter was lowered to the ground.

As the royal couple advanced, the head of the household prostrated himself at their feet, so overawed he scarcely heard the Inca tell him to rise.

"Rise, my good man," he repeated. "I wish you to show me your house."

But the king's men had to lift him to his feet. He was shaking like a leaf in the wind.

The Inca stooped to enter the door, protecting his red plumes with his hand. The inside was dim. In one corner were huddled a sick old man, the wife and the children, the youngest still at her breast. Dried meat and strips of chile peppers hung from the ceiling. In another corner were the work tools, the digging spade, the weed hoe, and the clod breaker.

As the royal pair advanced, the *cuyes* scurried off squeaking but soon ran back in. One of the smallest children crawled toward the emperor, and the frantic mother threw herself on him. "Let him crawl," said the emperor, "and nurse your baby."

His attendants brought in gifts, llama-wool cloth and potato flour. "Hereafter, you may call yourself an Inca," he told the shaking host.

The litter moved away swiftly. It paused in the village while the Inca listened to the local *sinchi* and gave him instructions. Outside the village the Inca descended from the litter again to pray at the wayside shrine.

The villager became a great man in his village. His whole life was transformed.

The Llama

Among the most important achievements of the Incas was to domesticate the llama, that camellike creature of the Andes. The llama lived in Peru before the Incas and throughout the empire at its greatest extension, and they live there still. The creature had flourished in Pleistocene times, before man appeared in the New World. The prehistoric llama had five instead of four toes, and a few of this breed still survive in the northern coast mountains.

Without the llama it is doubtful if the Inca empire could have been established. The Quechuas were largely dependent upon this animal for survival. It ministered to his need for warmth and clothing, his food, his health and spiritual life, and to carry his goods. On the basis of human and llama transport, the Incas built up a great flourishing trade.

The royal herds were sometimes as large as ten thousand head. Special officials managed the herds and kept a record of them on the *quipús*. A large number of skilled herdsmen were employed. At certain times llamas were given to high provincial officials and officers; and sometimes after a victory a pair might be presented to the most heroic fighters.

Some herds were reserved for the priests and for sacrifice on the altars. Nearly always black llamas were sacrificed. They were considered more perfect than white or brown llamas, for the latter had black noses, which were considered to mar their appearance. However, the Collas and Aimaras preferred to sacrifice white llamas. In the Inti Raimi ceremony in June, pure black llamas were sacrificed along with lizards, toads, serpents, foxes, jaguars, pumas, and many birds. At Coricancha in Cuzco every morning a white llama was sheared and sacrificed with a stone or copper knife. Other llamas were sacrificed for the *huacas,* or local shrines, and also for burial grounds. A llama was often buried with the dead for food on his long journey to the hereafter. The llamas were protected by various constellations—males by Lira, and females and their young by Cygnus.

A stele depicting Viracocha, God of the Sun

The Supreme God

Viracocha, the Sun, after whom an Inca was named, was the supreme god of the Incas, the ruler of the universe. In Cuzco the Sun was represented by a great jewel-encrusted slab of gold which blazed in the early morning sun. The people prayed to him for health and strength, good harvests, the fertility of the fields, and for victory over disease, misfortune, and enemies.

Garcilaso described him as the sole adored universal god, "who by light and power creates and sustains all things on

earth." He was the natural father of the first Inca, Manco
Capac, and his wife, Mama Ocllo, and all their descendants sent
to earth to benefit the people.

Chronicler Cristóbal de Molina recorded nine Quechua
prayers for Viracocha. Others were recorded early in the seven-
teenth century by Juan de Santa Cruz Pachacuti-Yamqui Sal-
camayhua.

O Viracocha. Lord of the universe,
Whether thou art male,
Whether thou art female,
Lord of reproduction,
Whatsoever thou might be,
O Lord of Divination,
Where art thou?

Thou mayest be above,
Thou mayest be below,
Or perhaps around
Splendid with scepter on thy throne
Oh, hear me! . . .
Oh, look down upon me,
For thou knowest me,
The sun—the moon—
The day—the night—
Summer—winter
Are not ordered in vain
By thee, O Viracocha!
They all travel
To their assigned places;
They all move
To their designed ends.

Inca Roca is said to have written:

Oh, come then,
Great as heaven,

Lord of the earth
Mighty First Cause,
Creator of men,
Ten times I adore you,
My eyes ever
Turned to the ground,
Hidden by eyelashes,
You I am seeking.

Actually the people felt more intimate love for the legend-
ary founder of their *ayllu,* or clan, and for many other lesser
gods, than for Viracocha, the majestic founder of the Incas,
who was always remote. Every family had its intimate
household gods, its lares and penates.

Sora Mama was the soul of corn, and many prayers and
sacrifices were made to her. There was divine Llama Mama
who looked after the herds. Miniature clay or stone llamas, with
a cavity in their backs for incense and offerings, were objects of
adorations to protect the herds. Offerings of *chicha,* brandy, or
coca leaves were made to them. Often they were buried in the
pastures between upright stones under a stone slab. Such stone
or clay llamas are still sold in the markets.

The god of thunder and lightning, or "gold splendor," was
depicted with club and sling, glistening as he whirled to strike
the heavens with storm, throwing out thunderbolts and bringing down rain and hail from the heavenly river, the Milky Way.
The hail was pictured as a puma eternally trying to devour the
sun and man. There were large temples to thunder and the
rainbow near Coricancha and today the chapel in the cathedral
dedicated to thunder and lightning is by far the most popular.

A panorama of earth is depicted in a circle with three
mountains and a red river under an arched rainbow. Another
panorama shows a heart-shaped area, labeled "Mother Lake,"
probably Titicaca (or perhaps the ocean) with a river connect-
ing it to a spring. In connection with it are shown seven circles,
"The Eyes of All Sorts of Things."

Among favorite gods for worship, the moon (Mama Quilla), the wife of the sun and queen of the sky, ruled over the winds, the sea and childbirth. Her temple was alongside the Coricancha. But it was not customary, according to Garcilaso, to make sacrifices to her. The god of thunder was considered more important.

The people made many offerings to the gods. Llamas and vicuñas, pumas, tapirs, *cuyes,* and birds. Special priests, under a lay director accompanied by a *quipú* keeper, performed all animal sacrifices. The worshipers might also place bird feathers, coca, corn, potatoes, *malanga, oca,* cloth, or gold and silver on the altars.

People carried on their persons small idols, or *huacas,* which they called brother or other endearing names. Some were in the form of serpents, birds, or animals and were often of gold or silver. That of Manco Capac was an *inti,* "sacred sun bird," a falcon which was kept in a basket. The personal *huaca* was buried with the owner at his death.

The sun cult was carried on by many devoted priests. The high priest, *uilac-umu,* an official of highest rank, sometimes a brother of the Inca, was the supreme arbiter in all religious matters. He appointed all priests and confessors (who prescribed penances) as well as inspectors who visited the temples and idols; and he supervised the *quipú* keepers. All the priests of the Sun in Cuzco were chosen from the original *ayllu* led to Cuzco by the first Inca. There were a dozen chief priests in the provinces who in turn had charge of the lesser priests and the oracles in the temples. Priests elsewhere were selected by local chiefs. The priesthood was often hereditary.

The high priest, a learned man, passed his days in religious contemplation and austerity. He was a strict vegetarian and drank only water.

His dark robe was ankle length. It had no belt or sleeves. Over it he wore a knee-length white, red-trimmed tunic covered with macaw feathers, jewels, and gold, a vicuña skull, and on his arms, gold bracelets. His shoes were of fine wool. For temple ceremonies, he put on the great crown with a round gold plaque representing the sun and, under his chin, wore a silver half-moon. His headdress was adorned with large macaw feathers, jewels, and slabs of gold.

Diviners and soothsayers dressed in gray garments and lived on herbs and roots. They were unmarried. Divinations were made with coca leaves and by coca chewing, with llama intestines, with spider legs and corn kernels. They often called the mountain spirits to assist them.

The Holy Vestals

Nuns served the cult. The Chosen Women, *ñustas* or Sun Vestals, were the most beautiful girls chosen by royal inspectors from all parts of the realm. They were from eight to fifteen. Every group of ten was in the charge of a *mamacuna*, guardian and mentor.

Convents for them were scattered far across the empire. In Cuzco the *ñustas* lived in a vast edifice *acllahuasi* of fine masonry, three hundred feet from the Coricancha between the temple and the Joy Plaza. It had a single door at the narrowed end and contained large halls, dormitories, workrooms, and storerooms. Each of the three thousand nuns had a servant. Each served a novitiate of three years, learning to sew, weave, cook, bake bread and cake, sweep and clean, and tend the sacred fire. Many daughters of the nobles were trained by the nuns.

After the three years' apprenticeship the *ñustas* were called *huamac* and were brought before the Inca. Those disinclined to continue their service were provided with husbands. Those who remained were dressed thereafter in fine white garments with garlands of gold, were called Sun Vestals, and continued to serve the Sun all their lives. They were always accompanied outside by an armed guard. Many fled when the Spaniards came, but some became wives of officers.

They were visited only by the *coya,* or queen, and her daughters, though legend has it that the Inca sometimes sneaked inside in the dead of night. His favorite nun served as the dictator of the establishment. A Sun maiden who sinned with lesser mortals was to be burned alive, her partner strangled.

Friar Alonso Ramós Gavilán mentions the *acllahuasi* on the Sun Island in Titicaca where the inmates were divided into three categories, according to their beauty and the tints of their skins, from white to red-brown.

The Solar Year

Religious fiestas were and are of great importance. The most important was Inti Raimi, the winter Sun festival, which marked the beginning of the June solstice. The exact time was determined by two sets of eight tall shadow-throwing towers in the mountains on either side of the Cuzco plain.

The ceremonies in Cuzco were presided over by the Inca and the *uilac-umu,* head of the church. There gathered the high-ranking *curacas, sinchis,* and governors of the provinces who came with impressive retinues. On the great days they wore puma skins, bright bird capes, fine-woven cotton of many colors. Mountain chiefs wore condor costumes with outstretched wings. There was a constant din of music from syringes, trumpets, shell horns, drums, and rattles.

A three-day fast preceded the celebration, followed by a feast. The night before the banquet the Chosen Women prepared corn bread or corn pudding. At dawn the Inca, in magnificent attire, headed a procession from the palace to the Joy Plaza where he and the important personages lay down flat, their faces toward the rising sun. They kissed the sunbeams. Lesser personages prostrated themselves in the Plaza of Sorrow nearby.

"Presently," wrote Garcilaso, "the king rose to his feet, the

Schoolgirls wait for classes to begin

rest still prostrate, and from two full gold cups drank *chicha* (made by the Vestals) . . . and invited all his relatives to drink in honor of his father, the Sun. He repeatedly emptied the cup in his right hand into a gold urn through which the liquor flowed by a conduit to the temple of the Sun to be drunk by the Deity. He himself drank from the cup in his left hand. . . . What remained, he divided among the nobles, pouring it into other cups of gold and silver."

The *curacas* in the next plaza drank the same beverage, then all marched in procession to the Coricancha. All but the emperor removed their shoes when within several hundred feet of the edifice. The Inca removed his at the portals. Only he and his relatives, the highest nobles, entered.

The priests received the gold cups from them and collected the others from the *curacas* outside, together with the offerings they had brought.

"Their gifts," said Garcilaso, "were . . . lizards, toads, serpents, foxes, tigers, lions, many kinds of birds . . . animals of the provinces imitated in miniature from nature in gold and silver."

Inside, a black llama was sacrificed. The animal's head was placed to the east, where the sun rose. Four nobles sat upon it while its left side was slashed by the priest, who pulled out the heart, lungs, and gullet. If the lungs still palpitated, it was a good omen. Otherwise a second or third llama was sacrificed. Other animals were also sacrificed, their hearts and blood offered to the Sun, and their bodies burned on a fire started by the high priest directing a beam of light from a concave metal plate on a small pile of wool till it caught fire. If the days were overcast—a bad omen—fire was made by rubbing hardwood sticks together. The meat of the sacrificed animals was distributed among the people along with corn bread and other food. After that there was much *chicha* drinking. The fiesta continued for nine days.

So began the solar year. In their calendar, they correlated it with the lunar year by scattering six extra days between the months. Then to round out the solar year, they added five extra days, called *allcan canqui,* "You are missing."

Late in June the old Inti Raimi fiesta is still celebrated on Sacsahuamán, the hill above Cuzco, with Quechuas taking the role of Inca and his attendants. A llama is still sacrificed, though not in the old Coricancha. It coincides now with St. John's Day. John the Baptist is the patron of sheep, and bonfires are built and sheep are branded, then brought to the church to be blessed.

The Month Fiestas

The June-July solar fiesta was in the first month.

Chahua Huarquiz, the second month (July-August), was devoted chiefly to celebrations of plowing, cleaning, and repairing irrigation canals. Inca Roca personally made offerings to the main spring when it was almost dry. He plunged his arm into the water, and thereafter it gushed forth abundantly.

Yapaquiz, the third month (August-September), was taken up with sowing crops, which called for special rites. Fifteen brown llamas were sacrificed. The state lands were plowed with special priestly rites. The priests themselves and the Chosen Women and their servants did much of the work. During this period the priests refrained from chewing coca and ate only unsalted herbs and toasted corn. A white llama, with gold ornaments in its ears, served as mascot. Much *chicha* was sprinkled on the soil. When the fields had been planted the llama and hundreds of *cuyes* were sacrificed. Corn, coca, bird plumages, and other offerings were made.

A moon festival called *Situa* was celebrated in *Coya Raimi,* the fourth month (September-October), to ward off sickness. All dogs, deformed people, and visitors from the provinces had to leave the city.

A great gold urn, guarded by four hundred warriors, was set up in the center of the Joy Plaza to receive *chicha* libations,

Unusual markings denote women and children of the upper Amazon who have come into town

which ran to the temple through conduits. In silence the people waited till the moon appeared, then burst into chants, "O sickness, disaster, misfortune, and perils go out of the land." The warriors made concerted charges shouting, "Go away, all evils, go away." The Inca and nobles joined in the chant, "Go forth, evil."

At midnight they went to bathe in the river carrying fireworks (as they still do today). They greeted the day with smiles, since all their aches and pains and illnesses were presumed to have been washed away. Mummies were carried to the banks to be washed, then smeared with corn gruel. People also smeared their faces with corn gruel, sprinkled some on the threshold and over all the niches where food was kept, and on all fountains.

A great banquet was set out. Portions of each dish were offered to the household gods. After the meal much *chicha* was drunk.

The people put on red tunics and carried their household gods and ancestral mummies to the plaza to dance. Feasting and drinking continued throughout the day. Frequent libations were poured into the golden urn for the gods and the priests.

The provincials were invited back into the city, bringing thirty white llamas to be burned on bonfires of aromatic wood. The animals' blood was used to make blood pudding and bread, which was distributed to the Chosen Women. This ceremony was held in all parts of the realm.

In the *Uma Raimi,* the dry fifth month (October-November), corn *chicha* was drunk and a black llama was "tied to the Sun," without being given food or water to oblige the god to send rain for it to drink.

The sixth month (November-December), *Ayarmarca,* was utilized for preparing boys for the important puberty ceremonies the following month when they were initiated as adult warriors. They went for a day and a night to high Huanacauri Hill some twenty miles from Sacsahuamán, where long ago one of Manco Capac's brothers had been turned into stone. Each sacrificed a llama and daubed the blood on his face. They returned with bundles of straw to provide seats for their relatives at the ceremony. The boys aided in making *chicha* by chewing the hard corn kernels to which was added water from a special spring.

The ceremonies ran over into the next month, *Capac Raimi* (December-January.) On the terrace of the Colcampata Palace the youths were instructed in the making and using weapons of war, sandals, and equipment. They were initiated by tests of virility, agility, and strength. After a week's near fasting on corn and water, they were fed a full meal. The final test was a race down from Huanacauri to the exercise plaza facing Sacsahuamán, where they were received in state by the Inca on his polished throne, surrounded by his entourage. The winner was made captain, and the first ten were commended for their swiftness and endurance. The less agile, slower ones were jeered at and forced to wear black loincloths instead of the white feather-trimmed ones provided the heroes.

The boys separated into two groups and a simulated attack and defense of Sacsahuamán was made. There were floggings and other tests of ability to withstand pain. If the Inca's son was among the contestants, he was given the severest tests of all. Costume dances continued to the point of exhaustion.

At the formal ceremonies, when the ears were pierced, the Inca inserted gold pins to keep the apertures open, the boys were dressed in their loincloths, given sandals and weapons, and garlanded with lily-shaped yellow, red, or purple flowers and wreaths.

In the eighth month, *Camay* (January-February), the new military corps went through prolonged, difficult maneuvers. They pelted each other with fruit (rather than stones) from their slings and engaged in hand-to-hand struggles. They were uniformed in black tunics, brown capes, and white feathers. The Inca supervised these exercises and signaled the end of them. The young men were cheered and given a feast.

On the first day of the new moon, during this same month,

Quechuas walk along the mystical Island of the Sun, overlooking Lake Titicaca

old llamas were brought in. Their ears were pierced and distended and they were provided with insignia meaning the "old chief."

At full moon llamas of all colors were sacrificed for the health of the Incas. An all-night dance in all the streets and plazas was celebrated, clothing was burned in adoration of the sun, the moon, thunder, and earth.

Toward the end of the month the images of the gods and the mummies were paraded by the priests. The people took hold of an enormous, long, thick, bright-colored cable, women on one side, men on the other, and moved in a tightening circle until they were compact. They then let the cable fall, coiled on the ground like a great serpent. Toward the heyday of the empire, the gold adornments on the cable became more numerous. Eventually a chain of pure gold—a rush order to the artisans—was substituted. A symbolic drowning of a gold chain in Lake Titicaca was made.

The rainy ninth month, *Hatún Pocoy* (February-March), had five fiestas. During the tenth month, *Pacha Pocoy,* the important Fire Fiesta was held. The last two months were harvest months. During *Arihuay,* the eleventh month, the puberty ceremonies for girls occurred.

In the last month, *Hatún Cuzqui,* which ended June 23, five llamas and other animals were sacrificed. As a sacrament the flesh was eaten raw in small chunks. In Sausera (modern San Sebastián) south of Cuzco, from the Track of the Sun, a farm belonging to the church, newly armed warriors in their best uniforms brought in the first of the crop in large bags, marching to music and singing lyric songs. The next day the nobles themselves brought in the rest of the crop and then replowed the fields till the sun sank in the western mountains.

So ended the Quechua year. So lived the Incas and their people.

Where the Incas Came From 6

The numerous ancient chroniclers tell many legends about the origins of the Incas. Sometimes the shining mantle story, mentioned in the first chapter, is told about Sinchi Roca, the second Inca of the Cuzco dynasty—the son of Manco Capac and his sister–wife Mama Ocllo.

The most accepted story is that Manco Capac, one of four brothers, was deposited by the Sun on an island in Lake Titicaca, that great inland sea fourteen thousand feet high, in the Andes.

Various writers, however, hinted at more ancient forebears. Chronicler Blas Valera, who was born in Peru, says that the royal dynasty began with Piruna Mancco, 1300 B.C., long before Cuzco. Others claimed the ancestors of the Incas came from Ecuador; others, from the Peruvian coast; and still others believe they were merely the chiefs of a small potato-growing Quechua *ayllu,* a family clan of llama herders, not far from Cuzco.

Manco Capac had the snake-oil salesman's talent to provide himself with a divine origin—certainly not the first nor the last religious prophet to be consumed by holy visions. Chronicler Garcilaso says that the four brothers, bearing the clan-name Ayar—Manco Capac, Cachi, Ucho, and Anco—and four sisters set forth from the holy Titicaca Island. Other writers said they were children of a sorceress who lived there, that Manco did away with the other brothers by turning them to stone. Mama Ocllo, one of the sisters, became the first empress.

Another sister, Mama Huaca, was warlike and blood-thirsty. She drove out Copalimayata, the king of the six *ayllus* already residing at Cuzco. He fled into hiding, leaving as his last message to his people that they were to remember him when-ever they looked on the sunlit snow in the high mountain passes, for there his soul would be dwelling—a bleak but beauti-ful conception.

Like the Aztecs far to the north in Mexico, the Incas were merely the latecomers into the land, who took over the cultural growth of ten or twenty centuries and forged the whole Andean world into a great and prosperous state.

Archeologists, as yet, have done little to establish the Inca period's links with earlier cultures, but great civilizations rose and fell thousands of years before on the coast and in the highlands. The Incas inherited their cultures and techniques.

The First Great Early Civilization

Chavín, the most remarkable and widely diffused early culture, radiated out from Chavín de Huantar in the white range of the Andes—Cordillera Blanca.

The time when Chavín was first settled, its impressive edifices constructed, its arts and sciences developed, the dates of the diffusion of its culture far and wide have been the subject of acrimonious disputes among the authorities. But ever since Julio C. Tello, for decades the dean of Peruvian archeologists, led his first expedition there in 1919 and later found evidence of the spread of Chavín culture to scores of sites along the coast and in the highlands of Peru and Bolivia, the accepted chronology of the rise and spread of the various civilizations has had to be reassessed.

Carbon datings of bones and charcoal found in the upper Mariñón region, as in the caverns of Lauricocha by Augusto Cardich, have provided dates of slightly over ten thousand years. The practice of agriculture dates according to locale from nearly 5000 to 3500 B.C. The building of Chavín's remarkable edifices probably postdates that achievement and must have required some centuries.

Up until sixty years ago the existence of Chavín was practically unknown, for over the centuries it had been repeatedly hit by earthquakes, landslides, and floods. It was almost buried and was finally abandoned by the early peoples. This is the same region where the terrible 1969 earthquake wiped out whole cities and left fifty thousand dead.

However, four centuries ago chronicler Pedro de Cieza de León mentioned the carved faces and human figures there, all "beautifully adorned." In 1624 another writer, Antonio Vásquez de Espinoza, compared it to Rome or Jerusalem. The great Italian naturalist Antonio Raimondi, in the 1870's, described a gigantic stele that depicted the "supreme deity." But most of the old city was still deeply buried, and Chavín was remote, in a wild gorge deep in the Andes.

Tello saw with excitement that it was the greatest discovery yet made in Latin America and not, as had been surmised, an extension of Central American or Mayan culture. Its very age indicated that it was a local evolution, older than the great early city of Tiahuanaco, south of Lake Titicaca, older than Chan-Chan and Mochica, or Nazca and Ica developments on the coast. There was a suggestion, since all the stone-cut Chavín motifs except the condor were from jungle plant and animal life, that the early city was founded by people from lower down the Amazon area, perhaps by the Arawaks whom Columbus found also in Cuba.

The mighty bird, the condor, has filled Peruvians with wonder through the ages. Its lofty flight reaches the summits of the highest 24,000-foot mountains. To this day in Huan-cavelica, the rose-colored mining town in the southern Andes, the people celebrate an annual condor dance, with masks and feathers attached to their arms they imitate the bird's soaring flight, its long glides, its swift descent and pouncing attacks of beak and talons on prey.

Magnificent stairways adorned with carved birds, serpents, fish, lizards, and a large jaguar-demon led from the lowest terrace up to the Holy Plaza, paved with polished stone, where stood the tall Lanzón, a twelve-foot stele of green diorite, depicting a symbolic feline head surrounded by snakes. Other stairs led up to a third terrace before a massive temple with two towers, from which animal heads and a frieze of jaguars, condors and snakes were projected. Inside the temple, the Raimondi Column supported stone roof slabs amid a labyrinth of dark galleries and chapels, with carved animals and birds, alabaster urns, and carved stone chests.

Spreading the Chavín Culture

Tello and others found that the early Chavín culture had flourished through all the upper Marañón (Amazon) headwater areas and down to the Pongo de Manseriche in northern Peru where the river bursts through the last Andean barrier, a location vividly and charmingly described by Ciro Alegría in his *The Golden Serpent*. At least ten Chavín centers were discovered, and in the Huaylas Callejón, a deep Andean canyon about nine thousand feet above the sea, at least four hundred large statues were found. On the upper Cotosh River, an Amazon tributary, Tello found plates and bowls with flat bases, oblique rims, and geometric and animal designs. Near Cajamarca in Cuntur Huasi, he uncovered a beautiful temple and stele with four magnificent statues, plant and animal figures, and symbol-adorned altars, and a massive stone aqueduct, profusely carved with Chavín inscriptions. The whole mountainside was terraced

The majesty of the main plaza in Quito reflects the great Inca palaces of long ago

with stone parapets filled with loam, much like those later built by the Incas. Tombs in the nearby Las Ventillas cemetery were carved out of solid rock, with several short personages seated among gold plaques incised with six large snake designs. Turquoise jewelry and a gold necklace were found together with a clay cup for the prolonged afterlife journey.

Chavín culture, it was found, by excavating below more recent structures of the last two thousand years, had spread all along the coast. The first such site full of astonishingly beautiful terra-cotta work was discovered in Cupisñique, north of present-day Trujillo, by the wealthy *hacendado,* plantation owner, Rafael Larco Herrera. It is thought—though later dates have been given—to have been started five thousand five hundred years ago. Carvings depict beans, potatoes, gourds, domesticated dogs, llamas, and jungle animals. Feverish explorations were made and similar sites were discovered in every northern coastal village. In northern Piura was found an exquisite tall vase with a round flared base and geometric designs. The vase, narrowing upward, had twelve oval niches shaped with eye and bird-beak designs.

Near modern Trujillo at Cerro Blanco, underneath a Mochica temple dating from the time of Christ, three Chavín epochs were uncovered, with the topmost temple on a platform of split stone and conical adobe. The ruins were shaped like a gigantic condor with spread wings. Walls were covered with red, yellow, and black stucco; sometimes a single enormous stylized bird or animal was depicted.

A Chavín-style settlement was discovered south of Lima at the seashore, with mat-rolled mummies and red-painted skeletons, also fishing gear, maize, yucca, and beans.

The early Chavín people wore loincloths, richly adorned capes, ornaments, beads, and necklaces of bone, and marvelously carved shells and stones. Those on the coast or in the highlands were adept at carving and sculpturing granite, quartz, porphyry, turquoise, lapis lazuli, shells, bone, and wood. Anthracite coal was polished for mirrors. Gold reliefs often imitated stone carvings.

Well south of Lima at Nepeña, superb edifices, with relief murals, are on superimposed platforms. A Chavín construction at Puncuri, also in the south, is pyramidal, above split-level platforms, reached by jaguar-guarded stone staircases.

The Paracas necropolis in Chavín style, with more than five hundred graves on Cerro Colorado above Pisco Bay, covers thirty thousand square feet. Numerous buried underground living quarters opened onto a series of patios that lead to the graves. The earliest ones, hewn out of red porphyry, were extensive underground chambers three yards deep. The well-embalmed mummies, seated in baskets, were wound in sixty yards of mummy-cloth and bore adornments of bone, shell, and gold of exquisite workmanship. Tello recorded the objects in one burial chamber: twenty-two shrouds, one human hair wig, feather fans, thirty-seven aloe fiber rugs, one stone club, three gold dishes, green, yellow, and red cups, shell bracelets, and strips of tanned leather. The garments under the shrouds, tunics, skirts, sandals, and coins (according to Tello) are still in good condition after thousands of years. From the skulls it can be observed that the early Chavín people performed brain operations by trepanning or cutting windows through the bone with obsidian knives and replacing the openings with gold plates.

The trail of Chavín discoveries leads on to remains in Cuzco, Ayacucho, Arequipa, and in Moxos in Bolivia. Square-edged reliefs at Tiahuanaco, near Lake Titicaca, suggest Chavín influence. Thus, the Chavín area was almost coextensive with Andean civilization thousands of years later.

Craftsmanship

The Chavín temples were built by talented and most likely well-schooled architects, artists, and artisans. Architecture, sculpturing, ceramics, and metal workmanship were superb. Artifacts, mortars, and chests of granite, onyx, alabaster, turquoise, quartz, and slate were beautifully designed and carved

with condors, jaguars, serpents, birds, sun, moon, and stars. Fine gold work—earrings, finger rings, nose rings, bracelets, plaques—have been unearthed at Chavín, Paracas, and Cuntur Huasi.

Carved animals were often provided with human heads and appendages. These were messengers of Oncoy, the supreme being. At their feet are plants, produce—fruits, manioc, peanuts, cotton, chiles—of the hot-land forests. Humanized bird heads have serpent or jaguar-claw hairknots. Feathers circle the eye sockets; face wrinkles are stylized snakes. Humanized jaguar heads have long, sharp teeth downward over the jowls. Humanized snake heads have triangular, hungry tongues and fangs. These formalized shapes symbolized the identity of humans with all creatures and supernatural forces.

The supreme deity Oncoy was a combined male-female lizard-dragon and jaguar. All in all, Oncoy was a fantastic and beautiful mélange of humans, tigers, mythical demons, decapitated heads, and sun faces. In the stone replica Oncoy bears on his back a human figure, who touches ten fingers to the dragon's tail. Oncoy's paws are jungle fruits, vegetables, and cotton. Interlocking teeth line his clearly depicted inner gastric tube to indicate his colossal appetite. Ahead of him fly three eager messengers—a jaguar, a parrotlike bird, and a river fish. The whole massive figure provides an impression of tremendous power, ferocity, and velocity. It is a fusion of man, animal, plant, the earth and stars, the entire universe.

A homogeneous civilization with a highly developed concept of art, ritual, religion, and work, Chavín was the root of the great tree of Peruvian life, which later flourished in Paracas, Moche, Nazca, Chanca, and Cuzco. Few of the actual links have been established yet by the archeologists, who have scarcely tilled the field, but the artifacts, carvings, and shells suggest centuries of growth at certain periods on an imperial scale.

Spanish influence is reflected in the façades of these buildings in Quito

Between Chavín and Cuzco

The Chavín story carries on through the exquisite Mochican culture of more than two thousand years ago, and the remarkable peoples strewn along the Peruvian coast, with their colossal irrigation works, their temples and fortresses, their fine carvings and artifacts.

The Mochican culture and later Chimú development extended through twenty valleys from the Gulf of Guayaquil to Nazca in the south. Chan-Chan, the splendid Chimú city by the sea ten miles from Trujillo, was several miles in extent and was protected by parallel walls fifty feet high and seven hundred feet long. Within were elaborate temples, palaces, fortresses, storehouses, dwellings, workshops, and burial chambers. Some of the edifices were built above mounds surrounded by fine gardens. The grand Chimú's palace, with notable bas relief decorations and nearly five hundred rooms, was said to have been lined with gold. Many gold and silver adornments and gold statuettes were discovered in the graves, which were tumbled over, and still are to this day. The Spaniards are said to have taken $3 million worth of treasure from the tombs, and the total taken has been valued at more than $15 million.

The buildings were constructed of adobe which endured for so many centuries because there is no rainfall in the region. Much of the city's food supply was grown within the walls. Their diet was supplemented by fish. The inhabitants dammed salt marshes to grow *totora* reeds, used for baskets, mats, and the making of seagoing boats.

Twenty miles south of Lima is Pachacamac, more or less contemporary with Chimú, which later became an Inca holy city. A century before the Spaniards, the Inca built a temple to Viracocha. It was about 400 by 180 feet. The walls were decorated with impressive frescoes of animal and bird designs; the doors were encrusted with crystal, coral, and turquoise. Most of it has disappeared.

The Nazca civilization, south on the coast, is recorded in

A young girl in the hot coastal region

textiles, terra-cotta ware, carvings, weapons, and implements. A badly destroyed palace and its notable aqueduct are visible. Its ceramics are graceful and brightly polychrome.

Between these cultures and the early center of Tiahuanaco in the Bolivian highlands near Lake Titicaca there was much interchange and for a time very likely conquest by Tiahuanaco. The earliest people at Tiahuanaco may have dated back ten thousand years; though the massive constructions there are of two widely separated periods of later expansion, subsequent to the Chavín era.

Tiahuanaco I was a temple, a city, a period, a style, and a culture that also extended over a vast area. It, too, represented a mighty upward thrust of art, architecture, religion, social organization; a grand expression of early human genius and achievement. Only the main constructions have ever been excavated, and carved stones can be encountered at almost any depth.

Some three centuries ago two Tiahuanaco stone statues were excavated, renamed Saint Peter and Saint Paul and, as Christian saints rather than pagan gods, still adorn the facade of the local adobe Catholic church. In the sixteenth century Spanish *hacendado* Juan Vargas, desperate for money, was told by a friendly native all he had to do was dig, and he unearthed a fabulous store of silver benches and flagons, gold beads, bangles, and a huge gold human head.

By the time of the Spaniards, according to Pedro de Cieza de León and Bernabé Cobo, the people around Tiahuanaco had no legends telling who had built either the first or the later city.

Possibly, but not likely, the early builders were the Urus, the Water People below Titicaca, who to this day claim to be the oldest people on earth, and some anthropologists claim they originally came from Australia. "We are not men, we are more than men," they claim. More likely, the Tiahuanacos were ancestors of the present day Collas, or the widespread Aimaras who are found over much of the highlands. The ancient city was on a flat, treeless plain twelve to fourteen thousand feet high.

Townspeople walking in this small plaza in Arequipa

The ancient gateway of the Calassaya in Tiahuanaco, Bolivia

A coarse grass made llama and alpaca grazing possible; otherwise, even today all seems lifeless. The red adobe houses so blend with the color of the soil as to be almost invisible a short distance away. The harsh, cold climate, with poor soil and limited choice of crops—and those often blighted—make the reddish plain bleak under lowering skies—handicaps that make the Tiahuanaco culture all the more remarkable.

The first Tiahuanaco was built of soft red sandstone, whereas the hard volcanic anderite of the Tiahuanaco II period had to be hauled from great distances, a real achievement, for some blocks weighed a hundred tons. The stones are well dressed and fitted, usually with angular notches and copper clamps for snug fitting. The major construction is the Acapana, a stone-faced natural hill, topped by a fifty-foot stepped pyramid, surmounted by a reservoir and dwelling apartments.

But the most dramatic surviving feature of Tiahuanaco is the enormous Gate of the Sun, with the Weeping God, serving as the entrance to the massive Calassaya staircase. The rectangular entrance was cut from a single gigantic stone. The carved god, perhaps Viracocha, would indicate a tie-up with the later Incas. But more likely this was an early ruler. His widespread arms and his four-fingered hands clutch a spear thrower and a quiver with two spears. His elaborate tunic is fringed with puma heads. Behind is a frieze of personified birdlike figures in rectangular frames, all racing toward him, each with a flowing headdress and a staff, perhaps the royal symbol of authority granted to the messengers, who, like the Inca *chasquis* of a later time, ran over the early roads and mountains, bearing news or royal orders.

The links between Chavín, Tiahuanaco I, and Tiahuanaco II have never been clearly established, nor have those with Cuzco and the Incas, but the architecture and artifacts suggest a definite relationship.

Tiahuanaco and the surrounding people were conquered very early by the Incas, who were astounded by the massive stone structures, which they in turn were to surpass in Cuzco.

Inca Monuments

Though the Spaniards destroyed many buildings in Inca Cuzco in order to build another city on its ancient stones, enough survived to preserve much of the old-time glory. Probably the Incas first appeared in the valley around A.D. 1040 and set to work promptly to build their city. It is still the archeological capital of the Americas. The main outlines, the plazas, avenues, some of them narrowed by the Spaniards, still rule the contours of the city.

It was, of course, brimming with life and industry before the Spaniards came. Today it seems somber and ponderous, rather silent.

The old Coricancha temple, with its curved east wall second-story arcades, and bright colonial frescoes circling the inner patio, was converted into the Church of Santo Domingo. The Temple of the Moon, which contained the mummies of the *coyas*, and the Temple of the Stars are almost intact today. The rainbow temple and that of thunder and lightning are mostly in ruins. The later temple to Viracocha, west of the main plaza, was razed and the present greenstone cathedral, filled with historical objects and works of art, was constructed on the massive foundations. Though stones from the ruins were used, by the time it was completed in 1564, the Viceroy Marqués de Mancera exclaimed it would have been cheaper had it been built of solid silver. In 1572 Mass was said, over many protests, for the souls of the last Inca Vilcabamba, a puppet emperor set in place by the Spaniards who in the end conspired against them and was executed in the Cuzco plaza.

The old Cuntur Huasi palace, in which the Spaniards took refuge during a Quechua uprising, was replaced by the Church of Triumph in memory of their miraculous escape.

The Jesuit church, La Compañía, was constructed from the magnificent palace of Inca Huayna Capac on the south side of the Plaza de Armas. Its paintings commemorate the marriages of Spaniards with the daughters of Incan nobility. The Jesuits'

apartments, with two bronze entrance statues of Inca emperors, have been utilized by the University of Cuzco for a museum of priceless examples of Inca art, ceramics, textiles, and trepanned skulls. A Spanish painting represents *Coya* Ocllo, the wife of Inca Manco Capac, being killed for refusing to provide the conquistadors with information, a singular disregard of actual chronology. There is also an alleged painting of Garcilaso de la Vega.

Of the old palace of the Vestals of the Sun, only a few walls remain in the west side of Callejón Cristo, opposite the walls of the Huayna Capac palace. Most of the edifice was replaced by the Convent of Santa Catalina. The old Concha Palace, named after a wealthy Spanish businessman who lived there, is now used by a modern business concern. For years it housed the *intendencía,* headquarters of the military governor. The last Spanish *intendent* was taken prisoner in 1814 during the Independence wars when the revolt of Inca Pumacahua occurred. The present police headquarters, the prefecture, is in an ancient Inca structure with arches and columns. Many streets are lined with massive Inca walls, some with neatly tailored enormous stones. Inside many Spanish-looking buildings, Inca rooms and other early remains are to be found. The architecture of many centuries—three periods, Inca, Spanish and Independence— are often ingeniously intermingled.

Other notable Inca monuments and remains are found in the environs of Cuzco; old walls rise above the Huatanay River twenty miles out. On a farm above Laguna de Salinas, where salt was obtained, are an ancient cemetery, carved stones, and an Inca bath. At picturesque Pumpanco rises a beautiful building of hewn stone. Other remains can be seen in San Gregorio, on the opposite side of the river. Little is left of the Huamacauri, on the hill from which the famous races of the Incan youth to Sacsahuamán began. Near here are the remains of the home of the late emperor Tupac Amaru II, who headed a nationwide revolt in 1780 that almost ran the Spanish out of the country. Up a side ravine are the high stone walls of what was once

Great craftsmanship is displayed in the palace arcades of La Compañía, Arequipa

Remains of the spectacular edifices which once towered on Machu Picchu

*Detail of one of the ruins
at Machu Picchu*

Tiporo, the remains of house, baths, terraces, and a cemetery. The place had a magnificent view of the lofty snow peaks of Ausamayate and Salcantay, seventy miles away. Also north of Cuzco rises Sacsahuamán, the most stupendous of all Inca construction. The Urubamba gorge is full of Inca fortified towns, many of them never examined.

Shortly before entering the jungle one finds the cliff-perched ancient city of Machu Picchu, perhaps the most dramatic archeological site in the world. It is an enormous maze of buildings, palaces, courtyards, narrow passageways, stone steps, carved observation seats, and stone-faced farming terraces. It was first opened up about sixty years ago by Dr. Hiram Bingham, Yale anthropologist. Most of the artifacts found were women's jewelry, mirrors, cosmetics, wearing apparel; and it has been conjectured that this may have been the refuge of the Vestals of the Sun at the time of the conquest. It has some of the finest stonework of the empire. Especially notable are the white stones of the main temple. Many walls rise from the very edge of the cliff, scarcely distinguishable from it, and the waters of the Urubamba swirl below. The walls contain numerous niches for images of Viracocha and other gods. Mummies of prominent people were kept in a special chapel. In all there are 3,200 stairs. Scores of similar cities, some of them high in the clouds, ring Machu Picchu. Few have been examined to any extent.

Numerous Inca ruins ring Puno on Lake Titicaca. More than half a dozen stone towers remain, and on the Island of the Sun—the Island of Sacrifices—in the lake, from which the first Inca and his brothers and sisters are said to have set forth to found the empire, rises the notable Temple of the Moon, examined long ago by the eminent archeologist Adolphe E. Bandolier. The Quechuas and the Incas also made many pilgrimages to the island. Inca Tupac Yupanqui founded the port of Copacabana, as a stopover place. It is located on a western mainland peninsula and elaborate dances and fiestas commemorate the old days.

A mother and her children going home from the fields

In the north, aside from the almost inaccessible Chavín, which was pre-Inca, the most interesting locale is probably Cajamarca, the summer resort around the old baths of Atahualpa. These are still in use. The water comes out of the hot springs at a temperature near boiling. Three triangular stone seats were carved for the emperor from which he could review his forces and enjoy the scenery. The remains of his palace and fort can be visited including the room, twenty-two by seventeen feet, where the ransom gold was heaped up as high as his extended arm. A red stripe is said to represent the height of the pile. The Spaniards took the gold and executed him anyway.

The well-paved, well-drained Inca roads can still be seen at various points. Particularly good stretches may be seen on the road from Cajamarca to Chachapoyas.

And so, in the long shadow of ancient glory and greatness live the sadly exploited Children of the Sun. These descendants of the Incas are still sun worshippers, and perhaps their day in the sun may be close at hand. Hopefully, Peru, where the winds of new doctrine are blowing, in due course will regain the prosperous days of yore. The Inca empire was the crowning political unification of centuries, spanning more than five thousand years in which new inventions, engineering, and the arts and sciences opened up new horizons and attested to the progress of hundreds of generations. Thus the Inca world was based on the efforts, the hopes, the trials, anguish, and persistent endeavor and talent of thousands of years.

Bibliography

Alergia, Ciro. *The Golden Serpent.* New York: New American
    Library,1963.
————*Broad and Alien Is the World.* Chester Springs, Pennsyl-
    vania: Dufour Editions, 1963.
Beals, Carleton. *Fire on the Andes.* Philadelphia: J.B. Lippin-
    cott, 1934.
Bejar, Hector. *Peru, 1965, Notes on a Guerrilla Experience.*
    Translated by William Rose. New York: Monthly Re-
    view Press, 1970.
Birney, Hoffman. *Brothers of Doom: The Story of the Pizarros
    of Peru.* New York: G. P. Putman's Sons, 1942.
Dodge, David. *The Crazy Glasspecker, High Life in the Andes.*
    New York: Random House, 1949.
Flornoy, Bertrand. *The World of the Inca.* New York: Double-
    day & Co., 1958.
Kelley, Hank & Dot. *Dancing Diplomats.* Albuquerque: Univ.
    of New Mexico Press, 1950.
Locke, Charles O. *The Last Princess.* New York: W. W. Nor-
    ton, 1954.

Markham, Clements R. *The Incas of Peru.* Lima: Pacific Press, 1967.

Means, Philip Ainsworth. *Ancient Civilizations of the Andes.* New York: Scribner's Sons, 1931.

Mortimer, W. Golden. *Peru, History of Coca.* New York: J.H. Vail, 1901.

Prescott, William H. *Peru.* New York: 2 vols. Peter Fenelon Collier, 1898.

Quijano, Anibal. *Nationalism and Capitalism in Peru.* Translated by Helen Lane. New York: Monthly Review Press, 1971.

Steward, Julian H., ed. *Handbook of the South American Indian.* vols. 2, 3. Washington,D.C.: Smithsonian Institution, Bureau of American Ethnology, 1948.

Toor, Frances. *Three Worlds of Peru.* New York: Crown Publishers, 1949.

Van Hagen, Victor W., ed. *The Conquest of Peru.* New York: New American Library, 1961.

Index

About the author

Carleton Beals, a well-known authority on Latin America, has written over forty books and countless articles on the subject. He has traveled on horseback through Mexico and Central America and has crossed the Andes several times.

A Guggenheim Fellow, Mr. Beals has been a faculty lecturer at The National University of Mexico, The University of California, and The New School for Social Research in New York. He and his wife live in Connecticut.

About the photographer

Marianne Greenwood was born in Sweden and has traveled extensively in Europe and Latin America. Her superb photographs have appeared in journals and books published internationally, and she collaborated with Mr. Beals previously on LAND OF THE MAYAS: *Yesterday and Today*, to which this book is a sequel.